Manager's Guide to Freight Loss and Damage Claims

Manager's Guide to Freight Loss and Damage Claims

Colin Barrett

Published by International Thomson Transport Press
1325 G Street, NW, Washington, DC 20005

©Copyright 1989, International Thomson Transport Press
1325 G Street, NW, Washington DC 20005
All rights reserved. No part of this book may be reproduced without permission of the publisher, except for brief passages included in a review appearing in a newspaper or magazine.

First edition

Library of Congress Catalog Card number 89-085335
ISBN 0-87408-048-7

Printed in the United States of America

Produced by AAH, Seven Fountains, VA 22652 (~~703~~ 540) 933-6210

Contents

Forward		xi
1	Introduction to the Law	1
2	The Basic Standard of Carrier Liability	9
3	When Carrier Liability Begins	11
4	When Liability Ends	15
5	Interrupted Transportation	23
6	The Exceptions (I): 'Act of God'	25
7	The Exceptions (II): Act of a 'Public Enemy'	31
8	The Exceptions (III): Act of a 'Public Authority'	33
9	The Exceptions (IV): Act of the Shipper	35
10	The Exceptions (V):'Inherent Vice'	47
11	The Exceptions: The 'But-For' Rule	51
12	The Role of Negligence	53
13	Regulated v. Unregulated Carriage	59
14	Waterborne Transportation	65
15	Air Transportation	75

MANAGER'S GUIDE TO CLAIMS

16 Intermodal Transportation 81

17 Third Parties 87

18 Contract Carriage 91

19 Released Rates 97

20 Responsibilities of the Parties 105

21 Inspection 115

22 Salvage 117

23 The Value of a Claim 121

24 The Value of a Claim—Loss 123

25 The Value of a Claim—Household Goods, Etc. 129

26 The Value of a Claim—Damage 133

27 Delay 139

28 Conversion 145

29 Discounts, Allowances and Interest 149

30 Taxes 153

31 Freight Charges 155

32 Administrative, Legal, Etc., Expenses 159

33 Special and Other Damages 161

34 Claims 167

CONTENTS

35	Time Limits for Filing Claims	175
36	Carrier Processing of Claims	179
37	Litigating Claims Disputes	183
38	Evidence and the 'Burden of Proof'	189
39	Arbitration	197
40	Insurance	201
41	'Self Help'	203
42	Claims Against Bankrupt Carriers	209
	Index	213

For Eve.

And, as ever, Alexandra

Foreword

ACCORDING TO COMEDIENNE ANNA RUSSELL, THE TROUBLE WITH commentaries on the subject of grand opera is that they tend to be "written by grrreat experts for the edification of *other* grrreat experts"—"leaving the average opera-goer," she adds, "as befogged as before."

I think she might well have offered the same observation about writings on matters of the law.

Too often legal discussions seem to be (to coin a phrase) of the lawyers, by the lawyers and—most regrettable of all—for the lawyers. Even those that purport to be in "plain English" wind up so riddled with legalistic phrasings and case citations that the lay reader is soon gasping with the effort to keep up.

Now, the average person can probably muddle along without ever fathoming the musicological intricacies of Wagner's *Der Ring des Niebelungen*; but when it comes to the law, a clear understanding of at least those aspects that touch on one's personal or professional life is pretty essential. After all, in order to observe and obey the law—duties our society imposes on everyone—one must first know what the law is.

In the transportation/distribution sector of the economy, one of the most troublesome areas of the law is that applicable to freight loss and damage. In the 16 years I've edited *Traffic World* magazine's "Questions & Answers" column, nearly half the inquiries I've received have dealt with aspects of this problem; and the vast majority of these seem to revolve around misunderstandings of the basic legal principles.

The purpose of this book (as its title implies) is to put those principles in the practical context of the transportation manager's day-to-day work.

It hasn't been possible to altogether get away from legalisms in writing this. Every discipline must evolve language to express the concepts unique to it, and you can no more write about the law without using some of its specialized jargon than you can write about mathematics without using numbers and symbols. But I've tried to minimize this whenever possible. So you'll find a *little* Latin, a *few* citations, the *occasional* legalistic phrasing—but not, I hope, so much or so many as to get in the way of clear communication.

In other words, this book isn't primarily for lawyers. It may be of some help to them—I hope it is—but its main purpose is to provide information to the transportation manager who has to cope with this area of the law without the benefit of a legal education or background.

The law is important to everyone. Q.E.D., *understanding* the law is important to everyone. I hope my efforts here can help promote that understanding.

                                                                Colin Barrett
                                                                March, 1989

1
Introduction to the Law

THE LIABILITY OF TRANSPORTATION CARRIERS FOR LOSS OF, DAMage to and/or delay of freight shipments is fixed by basic principles that are nearly as old as human civilization.

Indeed, the underpinnings of those principles date all the way back to times from which no written records survive. From the instant human society gave recognition to the concept of "chattel goods"—the legal term for one's possessions—it also had to face up to the complexities deriving from the fact that those chattel goods won't always be in the physical custody of their owner. That is, what happens if the goods should be lost or suffer injury when they are (temporarily) in another person's hands?

Over millennia the standards for resolving this question were refined into what has become known as the "law of bailments." In law, a bailment is "the relation created through the transfer of the possession of goods or chattels, by a person called the *bailor* to a person called the *bailee*, without a transfer of ownership, for the accomplishment of a certain purpose, whereupon the goods or chattels are to be dealt with according to the instructions of the bailor." In simpler (non-legal) terms, a "bailment" exists when one person has in his or her possession property that belongs to (is the "chattel goods" of) somebody else.[1]

The law of bailments defines the responsibility of the

---
[1] Dobie, *Bailments and Carriers* (St. Paul: West Pub. Co., 1914), p. 1.

"bailee" (the party holding the property) for loss or damage in such circumstances. Not unreasonably, this law varies substantially depending on the circumstances under which the bailee has possession of the goods. Thus, the finder of lost property assumes only an obligation of "slight" care for it, and only if he is derelict in this *de minimis* duty will he be liable if it is lost or damaged before its owner reclaims it. The borrower of another's property is invested with a higher duty to care for the goods, and hence assumes a greater degree of liability; the lessee may assume a heavier duty yet; and so forth.

Under first the customs and ultimately the written legal codes of antiquity, the strictest liability was imposed on those engaged in "common" callings—that is, those who, for hire, provided their services (in various capacities) to the public at large. Such persons were deemed to be "virtual insurors" of goods that came into their custody in the course of their businesses, liable for loss or damage under almost any circumstances *even if they were in no way at fault*. This standard was incorporated in the law of the Roman Empire, from which all western legal codes are derived.

In these earlier times, extending in many instances well into the Middle Ages, there was an extensive list of "common" purveyors on whom such liability was enforced. The common innkeeper, the common merchant, the common cobbler, etc., were just as liable for loss or damage as was the transportation carrier of that era.

Over the centuries, however, this list gradually shrank. In some cases the reason was simply the obvious unfairness of enforcing strict liability on certain classes of tradesmen; in others it stemmed from a view that property owners must assume greater responsibility for safeguarding their own possessions; and political and economic pressures (especially as exerted by medieval trade guilds) also played their role. The status of most common purveyors under the law of bailments gradually came to be that of an "ordinary bailee," held liable only where loss or damage resulted from his or her own negligence or culpability.

Thus, this strict liability has lingered on in modern times, a relic of history, only for the common transportation carrier. The rationale (or rationalization, if you prefer) for this is most famously explained in the legal case *Coggs v. Bernard*, decided in the year 1703 by one Lord Holt, a well-respected jurist of his time, who deemed it to be right and proper that transportation carriers should be "bound to answer for the goods [entrusted to them for carriage] at all events."[2]

"The law charges this person thus entrusted to carry goods [*i.e.*, the carrier]," wrote Lord Holt, "against all events but acts of God and of the enemies of the King. For though the force be ever so great, as if an irresistible multitude of people should rob him, nevertheless he is chargeable. And this is a politic establishment, contrived by the policy of the law for the safety of all persons, the necessity of whose affairs obliges them to trust these sorts of persons, that they may be safe in their ways of dealing; for else these carriers might have an opportunity of undoing all persons that had any dealings with them, by combining with thieves, etc., and yet doing it in such clandestine manner as would not be possible to be discovered. And this is the reason the law is founded upon in that point."

There are several noteworthy features of this admirably brief and cogent explanation. First, and most obviously, implicit in Lord Holt's comments is the fact that transportation carriers necessarily remove goods given over to them from the immediate geographic vicinity of their owner. It's a lot harder to keep your eye on your goods, that is, if the goods are (a) miles away from you and (b) in transit so that you may never be sure of their exact whereabouts from one moment to the next—and this was especially true three centuries ago, when Lord Holt wrote and when journeying even a few miles presented significant logistical difficulties.

---

2 2 Ld.Raym. 909.

Second, pragmatically speaking, the law of that era tended to extend not much further than the borders of the scattered townships and communities; the expanses in between were *de facto* a sort of no-man's land where force, rather than the civilized niceties of the law, prevailed. If Lord Holt's "irresistible multitude" of robbers were to strike, it was therefore more probable that they would do so away from human settlements—on the open road, where the goods they coveted were less protected. Such "highwaymen" as Dick Turpin and the latter-day Jesse James earned their notoriety, after all, mainly for robbing carriers, not shops or warehouses.

Third, as Lord Holt implied with his reference to "these sorts of persons"—one can almost visualize him delicately fanning away noxious odors as he wrote the words—common carriers of his era tended to be a pretty unsavory lot. To protect themselves against the hazards of that lawless open road they had of necessity to be fairly rough-hewn; and their integrity, as a class, was highly suspect. With no-one to see them do so, that they might "combine with thieves, etc. . . .in [a] clandestine manner" was not at all unlikely. Nor, as professional itinerants, did they have the kind of community ties and fixed addresses that might discourage them from following such a criminal path.

Yet, as Lord Holt touched upon, persons involved seriously in commerce had little choice but to deal with these carriers. Transportation has always been, and will always be, the cornerstone of trade; goods must be moved physically from the places where they're produced (which tend, due to the economics of scale, to be centralized) to the places where they're to be consumed (which tend to be dispersed)—and that requires transportation in some form or other. Because it's impractical and/or uneconomic for each producer of goods to operate his own means of transportation, the for-hire, or common, carrier is a logistical necessity.

Even these considerations, persuasive though they may be, don't entirely account for the strict liability vested in overland carriers. The selfsame things might also have been said of ocean carriers of Lord Holt's day; yet, even in that time, carriers by sea operated under a much less stringent regime of loss-and-damage liability (as remains the case today—*see below*).

It's possible, of course, to draw a bevy of distinctions between ocean and surface transportation, and to explain away the differences in their liability on this basis; and academicians who purport to see some sort of "grand design" in the law are prone to do so. But the fact is that this difference resulted mostly from the reality that seafaring carriers—especially in the ocean-minded British Empire, from the laws of which our own are descended—exerted a powerful political influence during the time when Lord Holt and other jurists were codifying the law of bailments, whereas their overland counterparts did not. Not surprisingly, they therefore received more lenient treatment under the law.

And once Lord Holt and others had established the precedents, the concept of common law that rules both the British and American judicial systems—the principle that yesterday's case is a binding guide to how today's is to be decided—made it exceptionally difficult to alter. Indeed, neither the nearly three centuries that have elapsed since the landmark *Coggs v. Bernard* ruling nor the Revolutionary War that made the United States independent from Britain (but left us with the heritage of its legal structure) have served to alter the main outlines of transportation liability law.

Is this to be interpreted as imputing an inherent validity to the legal standards that single out transportation carriers—alone among all other economic sectors—for such strict liability? In other words, are there, today, real-world reasons why carriers should be held more stringently liable than other bailees for loss of or damage to goods in their custody; and would we, if we were designing the law afresh today, incorporate into it such a standard?

Probably not. Most of Lord Holt's (and his contemporaries') concerns seem anachronistically out of place in today's world. The modern transportation industry has become an integrated and institutionalized part of our society and our economy, no less reputable or responsible than any other business sector; and there would appear to be no need, and no justification, for singling out carriers for such extraordinary liability.

Admittedly, there are those who disagree with this view. Their opinions were aired thoroughly during the 1980-81 investigation by the Interstate Commerce Commission into the liability question in response to a Congressional directive that a such a study be made.[3] In terms of operational consequences, the chief argument offered by those who opposed any reduction in the level of carrier L&D liability was (and is) that such a change would encourage carelessness on the part of the carriers in their handling of freight. If they were not held rigidly liable for loss of or damage to goods in their custody, they would tend to grow lax about taking precautions to prevent loss or damage for which they (putatively) would no longer be liable to the same degree as at present—or so, at least, goes the argument.

But it rings a bit hollow. For example, warehousemen, whose liability for loss and damage is limited to cases where they are negligent (or otherwise at fault), and who handle their customers' goods under circumstances similar to those obtaining for carriers, do not, as an industry, show a notably poorer record in this regard than do carriers. Moreover, it's fairly evident that, since no freight shipper wants his or her goods damaged while in transit, competitive pressures (especially under post-1980 transportation deregulation) are quite enough to deter carriers from growing sloppy about handling freight.

And indeed, at least during the early post-deregulation period this has largely been borne out. Deregulation has offered carriers a number of freedoms to reduce their L&D liability (*see below*); yet even those who argue most strongly against any

---

3 Incorporated in the Staggers Rail Act of 1980 as section 211(d).

changes in carrier liability standards acknowledge that, during that same span, loss-and-damage claims actually *declined*. At best, this argument is speculative and somewhat unconvincing, and the ICC, in its investigation into the subject, treated it as such.

Nevertheless, the Commission recommended to Congress that no essential change be made in carrier liability standards. It did so for a second, much more persuasive (and, in the final analysis, simpler) reason—that the present system is working effectively, and "if it ain't broke, don't fix it."

"[T]here may be some inequity in the present system," the Commission admitted in its report. But it also found that alternative approaches, such as a comparative-negligence standard (as applies to warehousemen and other "ordinary bailees") or some sort of "no-fault" system, incorporate their own built-in inequities—and lack, moreover, the great virtues of familiarity and the solid history of judicial interpretation and application that the present standards have.

In human society many ideas long outlast their usefulness. Dietary restrictions remain embedded in religious doctrine and/or social custom notwithstanding that technological advances in food preparation and preservation have rendered obsolete the hygienic concerns that gave rise to them. Coins are still faced with precious metals even though they no longer possess intrinsic value comparable to their denominations. And so forth.

The basic law governing transportation carriers' liability for freight loss and damage is another such fossil of social history. Though the reasons underlying it belong to an era long gone, it has become so entrenched a part of our society that it nevertheless continues to prevail without serious challenge. It's in this light that any study of the contemporary law of transportation loss and damage must be approached.

2
The Basic Standard of Carrier Liability

WHEN ONE PERSON—WHETHER IT BE AN INDIVIDUAL OR A CORporate "person"—transports another's goods as a common carrier, he is treated in law as the "virtual insuror" of the goods.

As the term "insuror" implies, this means the carrier must compensate the goods' owner for any loss of, damage to, or delay of the goods, *without regard to "fault" or "blame"*—pretty much as if it (the carrier) were a commercial insurance company. The carrier may have been altogether blameless; but if the goods were in its custody at the time, it must pay for the owner's economic loss.

As with insurance policies, however, there is some "fine print" in the law providing for such liability—some exceptions which exonerate the carrier from liability in certain circumstances. For surface overland carriers (the law is more lenient for air and ocean carriers—*see below*) there are five such basic exceptions to the strict rule of carrier liability:

(1) An act of God—a storm, a flood, an earthquake or some such similar natural calamity unforeseeable, and unpreventable, by human effort.

(2) The act of a "public enemy."

(3) The act of some public (*i.e.*, governmental) authority.

(4) The act, or omission, of the "shipper"—the term "shipper" in this context being defined broadly enough to embrace

both consignor and consignee, and even third parties who act as their agents.

(5) The "inherent vice" of the goods themselves—that is, their peculiar characteristics or nature which may render the loss or damage unavoidable.

To exculpate the carrier, one or another of these excepted causes (or more than one of them in combination) must have been the *sole* reason for the loss, damage or delay. Furthermore, the carrier must, in law, be prepared to *prove* that was the case. And finally, the carrier must not have been in any way negligent—lax or careless—in its handling of the goods, and must prove that, too.

This extraordinary level of liability attaches to the carrier only for such time as it has the goods in its possession *as a carrier*. If the carrier is acting instead in some other capacity—that of warehouseman, for example—it assumes for that span of time only the liability appurtenant to that other capacity, generally that of an "ordinary bailee."[1]

It has therefore become important over the years to define precisely when the carrier's status becomes that of carrier, subjecting it to the regime of carrier liability, and when that status comes to an end. And these events are *not* necessarily coincident with the carrier's assuming or relinquishing physical custody of the goods.

---

1   Also commonly called "warehouseman's liability." Warehousemen and other ordinary bailees are generally liable only for the consequences of their own negligence; and even then, if the owner of the goods is also shown to have been negligent, application of a "comparative negligence" standard may reduce the amount of such an ordinary bailee's liability or even serve to excuse him entirely.

3
When Carrier Liability Begins

COMMON CARRIERS ASSUME THE EXTRAORDINARY DEGREE OF liability imposed on them only to the extent that they have custody of the goods for purposes of transportation for hire.

In other words, if the carrier is not, at any given moment, functioning in its capacity as a carrier, its liability is only that of an "ordinary bailee" such as, for example, a warehouseman. This doesn't mean the goods must be physically in motion in order to invest the carrier with liability as such; the law recognizes that the transportation process necessarily involves periods of time when, for operational reasons, the goods will be temporarily stationary. But an ongoing transportation movement must be in process if the carrier is to be liable as a carrier.

"A carrier's liability attaches as soon as delivery to it is complete. . . . Delivery cannot be complete if anything remains to be done by the shipper before the goods can be sent on their way; but if the thing to be done is something which it is the dutyof the carrier to do, without further act on the part of the shipper, then the liability of the carrier attaches at once."[1]

The shipper's first duty, obviously, is to turn the goods themselves over to the carrier. But the transfer of possession need not be a direct one, and often isn't. Parcel carriers, for example, often maintain drop-boxes at various locations, have

---

1 *Corpus Juris Secundum*, 13 C.J.S. Carriers § 145(a).

standing arrangements with hotels, etc.; and the law provides that the carrier's liability attaches from the moment the goods are left "in the place at which they are accustomed to be deposited, or at a place specifically designated by contract [or tariff, rate circular, etc.]."[2] Rail cars are commonly left in place for the railroad to move out at its convenience, and the same standard applies—as it also does with respect to "drop trailer" pickups by motor carriers.

However, if goods are tendered to the carrier in this remote-control sort of way, the shipper must be careful to ensure that the carrier holds itself out as ready, willing and able to provide the transportation service required. The law specifies that, for the carrier to assume liability as a carrier, not only must the goods be given over to the carrier's custody but *the carrier must accept them for transportation*. Legal standards are plenty loose enough in this area to permit "implicit" acceptance by the carrier—that is, the carrier does not have to make a specific acceptance on each shipment—but they also allow for implicit *non*-acceptance in particular circumstances.

In general, carriers are permitted to restrict their services more or less as they see fit in terms of the traffic they will handle and the traffic they will not.[3] Some carriers, for example, "embargo" certain types of freight, or shipments moving to or from particular points or areas; they state publicly, usually in tariffs or rate circulars, that they won't accept such traffic. In other cases carriers are restricted in the service they can provide by economic regulatory standards, insurance requirements, limita-

---

2 13 C.J.S. § 144.
3 There are in fact certain limited exceptions to this rule; but the once-powerful "common carrier obligation" of the Interstate Commerce Act has been largely emasculated by administrative rulings of the Interstate Commerce Commission. The only realistic approach for the shipper is to consider that carriers' willingness to carry freight is limited to their "holding out"—that is, the service they offer, by advertisement, tariff, contract, etc., to provide—and be guided accordingly.

WHEN CARRIER LIABILITY BEGINS

tions of their operating equipment, etc. In yet others, involving interline shipments, carriers may not have proper through routes with one another to accomplish the transportation.

And if the shipper gives a shipment to a carrier that cannot, or has advised that it will not, provide the requested transportation service, the prevailing law holds that the carrier does *not* become liable as a carrier; because it is not functioning as a carrier with respect to that shipment, its liability is only that of the ordinary bailee. Thus, it behooves the shipper to remain alert to limitations in carrier service.

Of course, any *explicit* acceptance by the carrier of a particular shipment will ordinarily be considered as overriding such generic service limitations. Even if it ultimately develops that the carrier can't provide the requested service and must return the goods to the shipper, if the carrier specifically agreed to accept the shipment it will normally be deemed to have assumed liability as a carrier for the time it held the goods.

The shipper also has at least one further duty before the goods may be deemed to have been tendered the carrier for transportation (rendering it liable as a carrier): it must furnish the carrier with shipping instructions. The format of those instructions is unimportant, and even verbal instructions, if accepted by the carrier, will suffice; but the carrier can't commence transportation of the goods until it has the necessary information about where the shipper wants them hauled, any particular ancillary services required, etc., and is therefore not in a position to act as a carrier, or assume carrier liability, until it has that knowledge. In the case of shipments being made available for transportation on an "on call" basis, the instructions must also include the information that the shipment is ready to be picked up.

But although shipping instructions must be complete, it's worth re-emphasizing that *no specific form is required*. In particular, although shippers frequently provide such instructions in the form of a bill of lading, in law it is the *carrier's*, not the shipper's, obligation to issue bills of lading.[4] Therefore, under the general rule cited above, preparation of a bill of lading is *not* a precondition to the carrier's assuming liability as a carrier.

The shipper may also have still other duties to discharge before the goods are deemed ready for transportation. Where the shipper has not made advance credit arrangements with the carrier and the shipment is prepaid, for example, the shipper must tender payment; and the carrier's liability as a carrier does not commence until this has been done. Other responsibilities such as furnishing of documentation the carrier may require, etc., must also be discharged by the shipper before the carrier assumes liability as such.

Where the carrier receives the goods not from the shipper but from some other party—an agent of the shipper, a commercial third-party factor (broker, shippers' agent, forwarder, etc.), another carrier in interline service[5]—the same basic circumstances obtain; that is, the carrier must have the goods in its possession (or available to it) and complete shipping instructions before it assumes carrier liability with respect to the shipment in question.

---

4 Interstate Commerce Act, 49 U.S.C. § 11707(a); see also the Pomerene (Bills of Lading) Act, 49 U.S.C. §§ 81-124.
5 But see the discussion of "joint and several liability" of interline carriers below.

4
When Liability Ends

AT THE OTHER END OF THE TRANSPORTATION, THE CARRIER'S liability as a carrier ceases when:

(1) it makes physical delivery of the shipment to the intended consignee; or

(2) it makes a tender of delivery of the shipment to the consignee, but the consignee rejects or otherwise refuses to accept delivery; or

(3) the consignee fails to exercise "due diligence" in accepting proffered delivery of the goods within "a reasonable time."

When physical delivery is made, the precise moment at which custody of the goods passes from the carrier to the consignee can be critical, as illustrated by one case reported to the author. A parcel was being delivered in the garment district of New York City; as usual during business hours in that congested area, the truck could not pull up to a loading dock but had to park in the street. An employee of the consignee came out to the sidewalk, the driver removed the package from the truck and started to hand it to him.

At just that moment a young man riding a skateboard shot between them, snatched the package and fled, eluding pursuit. Liability for the loss—whether it had to be borne by the consignee or the carrier—was obviously contingent on whether possession of the goods had physically passed from the driver to the consignee's employee at the moment of theft, but since neither party could answer that question for sure, the case was severely muddled from a legal standpoint.[1]

Leaving aside such unusual circumstances, the moment at which delivery is deemed to have been made will depend on the terms of the contract of carriage (usually the bill of lading, including any tariff or rate-circular provisions incorporated into it by reference). As a general rule, the carrier must discharge all its obligations under the contract before delivery may be said to be complete. Thus, if the contract calls for the carrier to unload, it must do so before its liability as a carrier comes to an end; if inside delivery is required, that, too, must be accomplished; and so forth.

If, on the other hand, the contract specifies that the consignee is to unload, the carrier's liability as a carrier ends as soon as its vehicle is positioned where the consignee specifies. And in the case of rail shipments and some motor carrier drop-trailer deliveries, if the consignee is unable to accommodate the vehicle at its unloading dock the carrier may fulfill its obligation as a carrier by "constructively placing" the shipment on a rail siding, in a parking area, etc.

Of course, delivery arrangements can always be altered by agreement between the carrier and the consignee at the time of delivery; for example, the consignee can request, and the carrier agree, that the carrier perform unloading even though the original contract of carriage stated that the work was to be done by the consignee. In such cases, the carrier's liability as a carrier is extended until the additional agreed work is completed. It has been held that such an agreement may be binding on the carrier even if its tariff (or contract, rate circular, etc.) makes no provision for it to perform the added work.[2]

---

1 In the event, the parties agreed amicably to share the loss, and the case never went to litigation.
2 *Loveless Mfg. Co. v. Roadway Exp., Inc.*, 104 F.Supp. 809, citing *William Ramsey v. N. Y. C. R. R. Co.*, 199 N.E. 65; cf. *American Jurisprudence*, 9 Am.Jur. Carriers 467.

However, especially in the case of motor carrier shipments, consignees should proceed in this area with some caution. Even if the driver agrees to unload, he may in some circumstances be deemed in law to be acting independently, and not in his capacity as agent for the carrier—and in such circumstances the carrier does not incur additional liability (beyond what the original contract of carriage covers) by virtue of anything the driver may say or do.

Some consignees seek to require drivers to unload, or participate in unloading, coercively; that is, they will refuse to accept delivery, or will threaten to keep the driver waiting for extended periods before delivery may be made, if the driver doesn't unload (even though the contract specifies that the consignee will unload). Others, instead of the stick, use the carrot; they offer to "tip" drivers for unloading or helping to unload. In both cases they are sometimes successful in persuading the driver to do their bidding.

Such arrangements, however, may well be legally considered as private ones between the consignee and the driver, with the carrier not being a party to them and therefore assuming no additional liability as a result. Indeed, the driver in such cases may be considered to be acting as the legal agent of the consignee, *not* of his employer, the carrier; and since the carrier is therefore not responsible for the driver's actions or failings in such circumstances, this can have serious consequences for the consignee.

The author was told of one such case in which a palletized load of aerosols was delivered under a bill of lading with a "consignee unload" notation. Nevertheless, and notwithstanding that the carrier's tariff made no provision for carrier unloading of palletized freight, the consignee instructed the driver to unload, using a forklift on the premises. The driver attempted to do so, but in the process punctured some of the aerosol cans with the tines of the forklift; the friction of metal on metal produced sparks which ignited the flammable aerosol propellant;

and the ensuing conflagration consumed the shipment and the vehicle on which it was loaded and did additional damage to the consignee's dock. Yet the driver was deemed in this case to have been acting as the legal agent of the consignee, not the carrier, at the time this occurred; not only was the carrier free from liability but it was in a position to claim damages for the burned trailer from the consignee—even though its own employee caused the fire!

Alternatively, the carrier is relieved of liability as a carrier if it tenders the goods for delivery and the consignee refuses to accept them. The tender of delivery, however, must be a proper one; the carrier can't just show up on the consignee's premises late Saturday night. Delivery must be made during normal business hours; or, if the carrier has accepted a delivery appointment (as many consignees today require), it must arrive at the appointed time.

Because the consignee's rejection or refusal of the load will end the carrier's liability as a carrier, it is clearly unwise for consignees to take such action in normal circumstances. Obviously this subjects the owner of the goods to additional risk, since the carrier's liability for any loss or damage occurring *after* the rejection or refusal is limited to that of an ordinary bailee—*i.e.*, it is liable only for the consequences of its own negligence or other fault.

In fact, a general precept of the law is that the consignee has an affirmative obligation to accept delivery of the shipment, the tacit corollary being that he can be sued for damages resulting from his failure to do so. This holds true *even if the shipment is in damaged condition upon arrival*; "[t]he fact. . . that the goods were injured upon the journey through causes for which the carrier is responsible does not of itself justify the consignee in refusing to receive them, but he must accept them and hold the carrier responsible for the injury."[3]

---

3   3 *Hutchinson on Carriers* 1365.

The reality, however, is that few things in life rival damaged freight in unpopularity; many consignees have policies of refusing to accept delivery of such goods. This is certainly understandable from the consignee's perspective, but it overlooks the legal problems that can result. Among other things, freight that has already been damaged in transit is very possibly more vulnerable to further subsequent damage (because of injury to its protective packaging, etc.) than is undamaged freight. And in cases of consignee rejection or refusal of delivery, the carrier will only be liable *as a carrier* for such damage as may have occurred *prior* to the rejection or refusal.

Thus, if the consignee is deemed to be the owner of the goods at the time they are tendered for delivery—if, particularly, terms of sale were f.o.b. origin—he is risking loss or damage to *his* property for which he will have only a very limited right of recovery from the carrier. Even if circumstances are such that the consignee does *not* have title to the goods, if they're lost or damaged following a rejection/refusal and the carrier is not found liable, the goods' owner may possibly be in a position to sue the consignee for damages—and, since the consignee has in such circumstances violated its affirmative duty to accept delivery, such a suit could well be successful.

There are, however, three basic exceptions to the rule that the consignee must, in law, accept delivery:

(1) If the goods are so badly damaged as to be economically worthless, the consignee need not accept delivery. ". . . [W]hen the 'entire value of the goods has been destroyed and the injury amounts practically to a total loss'. . . the consignee is justified in refusing the goods. . . ."[4] In other words, no-one can be obliged to take delivery of what *de facto* amounts to worthless trash.

(2) There is, of course, no obligation that a consignee accept goods sent to it unbidden—that is, without having been ordered

---

4   *Wilkins v. A. C. L. R. Co.*, 75 S.E. 1090, 1092.

(including by "standing order") or purchased. This is a variant on the legal principle that allows consumers to refuse to pay for unordered items that arrive in the mail, by parcel express, etc. But it applies *only* to the unordered goods; if a shipment also includes some goods that *were* ordered or purchased, the consignee can't reject or refuse the entire load with impunity merely because a portion of it falls into the unordered category.

(3) Rejection or refusal should not be confused with reconsignment or forwarding of the shipment. The doctrine that ends the carrier's liability upon tender and refusal of delivery is based on the fact that these events have concluded its duties under the contract of carriage (bill of lading), and it is therefore no longer acting as a carrier *vis-à-vis* this shipment. If the consignee says, in effect, "Take it away, I don't want it," such is the case. But if the consignee instead says, for example, "Take it back to the shipper," or "Send it to such-and-such other place," he is in effect giving the carrier further, supplementary shipping instructions; and presuming those instructions are within the capacity and the "holding out" of the carrier, this serves to extend the contract of carriage and, concomitantly, the carrier's liability for the goods as a carrier. (Of course, the carrier may also charge for such further service in accordance with its tariff or rate circular.)

If the consignee does reject or refuse delivery without providing such further shipping instructions, the carrier's liability as a carrier ceases *as of that moment*. When its vehicle, still loaded with the freight, departs the consignee's facility, the carrier's liability is only that of an ordinary bailee; and that remains the situation until such time as the carrier is provided with new shipping instructions, at which time it becomes liable once again as a carrier since it is once again acting in that capacity with respect to the shipment.

The third and final circumstance under which the carrier's contractual obligation, and hence its liability, as a carrier, is deemed to have been terminated—when the consignee fails to exercise "due diligence" in accepting delivery within "a reasonable time"—gives rise to potential problems, especially in today's real-world transportation industry. The problems arise largely because of the inspecific nature of the phrases that are in quotation marks above—*i.e.*, what constitutes "due diligence," and what's "a reasonable time"?

The legal principle, and the court cases expounding and developing it, date back to a different era in transportation. The cases mainly deal with either (1) situations where the goods were to be held on the carrier's premises—*e.g.*, terminal or railroad team track—for consignee pickup, or (2) questions of "constructive placement" of rail cars due to congestion at the consignee's facility. Although determination of the specific meaning of "due diligence" and "a reasonable time" depend in such cases, too, on the individual circumstances of each case, there is considerable precedent available to help resolve any disputes.

But the increasingly common practice of consignees in requiring motor carriers to make delivery appointments in advance gives rise to the possibility of disputes for which there is apparently little or no precedent case law. What if the carrier calls for such an appointment and is told he can't have one until the next day? Two days later? Two *weeks*? At what juncture, specifically, is the consignee deemed to have failed in its obligation to exercise due diligence; when does the enforced delay in delivery become *un*reasonable; when, that is, does the carrier's liability for the goods as a carrier cease, to be resumed only when the day and hour of the long-awaited delivery appointment arrive?

Some carriers have, astutely, published in their tariffs and rate circulars rules which define the maximum allowable wait before a delivery appointment, after expiration of which storage and/or redelivery charges will be assessed. The probability (in light of the absence of case law this can't be viewed as a certainty) is that the courts would be guided thereby regarding questions of liability. But the absence of such tariff or rate-circular standards does not mean the delivery-appointment delay is unlimited; courts would most likely base decisions on what they could learn of industry practices, past custom in the particular shipper-consignee relationship (if any), etc.

A conservative approach to this question suggests that, to ensure uninterrupted application of the regime of carrier liability, a consignee should not ask the carrier to wait longer than overnight for a delivery appointment; and in some cases (where an appointment was requested far enough in advance to permit a morning delivery on the day in question), even that might be deemed excessive. Failure of consignees to abide by this standard could mean that, for the time it is waiting for the delivery appointment, the carrier may be deemed to have liability only as an ordinary bailee, not as a carrier.

Again, delivery to a party other than the consignee, such as a broker or connecting carrier,[5] is treated on the same basis as delivery to the consignee for purposes of defining when carrier liability ends.

---

[5] And, once more, see below for a discussion of the "joint and several liability" of interline carriers.

5
Interrupted Transportation

THERE ARE A FEW CIRCUMSTANCES IN WHICH TRANSPORTATION service will not be continuous in nature, either by original intent or as a result of circumstances that develop while the goods are in transit. Such "interrupted transportation" will produce a concomitant interruption in the carrier's liability for the goods in its capacity as a carrier.

As discussed (*see above*), the basic rule is that the carrier must have (a) custody of (or access to) the goods themselves, and (b) shipping instructions *which it is in a position to execute immediately*—notwithstanding that it may elect to delay such execution for its own convenience—in order to be held liable as a carrier. Where the goods' owner, or anyone else having the legal right to do so, directs that the transportation service be paused for some reason, this is, of course, no longer the case.

In some instances, especially as to household goods, the shipper will direct that goods be moved to a storage facility and held there for a period of time that may be fixed or indeterminate ("until further orders"). Even if the carrier also operates the storage facility, and thus retains physical possession of the goods throughout, its liability is that of a warehouseman while the goods are in storage. Only when the time comes (either predetermined or based on new shipping instructions) for their removal from storage does its liability as a carrier resume.

In a few industries it is common practice for shipments to be dispatched in advance of their actual sale. That is, they are set in motion in what the shipper believes to be the general direction of their expected buyer consigned either to an indeterminate or an artificial destination; a sale is transacted while they are in transit, and they are then diverted or reconsigned appropriately.

This process, which is intended to expedite delivery of goods to their buyers, ordinarily runs smoothly, and the diversion/reconsignment orders reach the carrier while the goods are still in motion; thus, the transportation is continuous and there is no interruption in the liability regime. On occasion, however, completion of a sale will take longer than the shipper has anticipated, and the goods will come to rest in a rail yard, truck terminal, etc. In such cases the carrier's liability as a carrier ends when they do so, and does not re-commence until the shipper has delivered new instructions for their further movement.

The owner of goods in transit also has the right of stoppage *in transitu*—that is, to direct an unplanned interruption in the goods' movement. For example, a customer order may have been unexpectedly canceled, the shipper may have belated doubts about the customer's solvency, etc. Carriers are obliged to comply with such directives; but unless they are accompanied by concurrent diversion/reconsignment orders, the carrier's liability ceases until it is given new shipping instructions or the owner rescinds the stop order so that the transportation may resume.

Some freight also moves under so-called "transit" arrangements by which it is hauled to an intermediate point for processing, assembly, partial manufacture, etc., and then re-shipped via the same carrier. For rating purposes the fiction is maintained that the entire origin-to-destination movement is a "through" one; but the carrier is of course not liable for the freight between the time of its delivery at the intermediate point and the time it is re-tendered for onward movement.

6
The Exceptions (I): 'Act of God'

"NOW WHAT IS AN ACT OF GOD?" RHETORICALLY ASKED ONE OF the earliest British jurists to deal with the legal standard that exonerates carriers from liability for loss and damage resulting from this cause.

"I consider it to mean something in opposition to the act of man; for everything is the act of God that happens by His permission, everything by His knowledge. But to prevent litigation, collusion and the necessity of going into circumstances impossible to be unraveled, the law presumes against the carrier unless he shows it [the loss or damage] was done by. . . such act as could not happen by the intervention of man, as storms, lightning and tempests."[1]

It must be stressed that, in order to qualify as an act of God in this limited legal context, the calamity must have resulted from demonstrably *natural* causes. To draw the distinction clearly, a fire caused directly by a lightning strike is considered an act of God; the same fire, if it resulted from some other, human-related cause—or even if its cause were unknown—would not be deemed an act of God insofar as excusing the carrier from liability for the resulting damage to goods in its custody.

The act-of-God exemption is, as the foregoing suggests,

---
1 *Forward v. Pittard*, 1 T.R. 27.

intended primarily to cover natural occurrences which are (1) unusual to a high degree; (2) unpredictable; and (3) of a fairly severe or dramatic nature. Thus, such events as earthquakes, tidal waves, lightning strikes, hurricanes, tornadoes and cyclones, etc., qualify, whereas ordinary thunderstorms, blizzards and the like generally do not.

But the dividing line cannot always be so neatly drawn. For one example, hurricanes are technically defined as storms featuring winds in excess of 70 mph, but this definition, while undoubtedly useful for meteorological science, cannot always be applied so rigidly in the case of loss-and-damage liability law. It would be ridiculous to suggest that a carrier would be liable for damage caused by winds of 69½ mph, but exempt from liability if the wind velocity were less than half a percent greater.

Moreover, the threefold test described above must be considered in the context of geography and the calendar. A winter snowstorm in northern Minnesota is not uncommon, and would generally not be considered an act of God for purposes of exempting a carrier from L&D liability. But such an event probably *would* qualify if it occurred in southern Florida, or even in Minnesota in mid-summer.

At the same time, the question of the unforeseeably exceptional nature of the event shouldn't be carried to extremes. In one case a shipper sought to override a carrier's claim to act-of-God exemption on the ground that a flood similar to that one that had damaged its (the shipper's) goods had occurred 85 years earlier; the court properly ruled that this did not deprive the more recent flood of its legal status as an act of God.[2]

Another factor that must be taken into consideration is whether the carrier, to the extent it had the opportunity to do so, took reasonable precautions to protect the goods in its custody. Some natural calamities occur with virtually no warning—earthquakes and tidal waves, for example. But in other cases there

---

2   *L. & N. R. Co. v. Finlay*, 185 So. 904.

may be some advance notice of the impending problem; hurricanes, for example, are tracked with extraordinary precision by weather forecasters, and those in their potential paths often receive widely publicized warnings well ahead of the storm's arrival. If a carrier fails to take reasonable measures to safeguard the goods in such cases—by protecting them, moving them, etc.—it may be held liable (on grounds of negligence—*see below*) even though the event itself was indisputably in the act-of-God category.

"It requires no citation of authority to sustain the proposition that, after a carrier has discovered or by the exercise of reasonable prudence and diligence should have discovered that goods in his possession are subject to the perils of an unprecedented flood or other *vis major* [literally, 'greater force'—here used as more or less a synonym for 'act of God' (*although see below*)], it is his duty to exercise reasonable care and diligence to save them from damage or loss."[3]

In addition, the act of God must be the *only* cause of the loss, damage or delay.

". . .[T]he notion of [this] exception is those losses and injuries occasioned *exclusively* by natural causes, such as could not be prevented by human care, skill and foresight. . . ," said one court. "If the loss or injury happen *in any way* through the agency of man, it cannot be considered the act of God; nor even the act or negligence of man *contributes* to bring or leave the goods. . . under the operation of natural causes that work their injury, is he [the carrier] excused.

"In short, to excuse the carrier, the 'act of God'. . . must be the sole and immediate cause of the injury. If there be any cooperation of man, or any admixture of human means, the injury is not, in a legal sense, the act of God."[4]

A case in the author's experience which illustrates this point

---

[3] *Ferguson v. Southern Ry.*, 74 S.E. 129; see also *The Majestic*, 166 U.S. 375.
[4] *Michaels v. N. Y. C. R. Co.*, 30 N.Y. 564; emphasis added.

had its inception in an unexpected flood that washed out a railroad branch line. The carrier elected, with the acquiescence of the only two shippers served by that line, to abandon the line rather than rebuild it; but it confronted the problem of retrieving two loaded boxcars stranded at the far end of the line. The cargo was a bulk commodity of such a nature that it could not be unloaded as the cars sat; and since the cars could not be physically moved with their lading (there being no power unit available), the cargo had to be dumped at that point and the cars removed by means of heavy highway equipment.

The railroad sought to escape liability for the dumped cargo under the act-of-God exemption. But although the flood itself was fairly clearly in this category, it was not the proximate cause of the shipper's loss; rather, the loss occurred only when the carrier dumped the cargo, which was obviously not an act of God in any sense.[5] As this case illustrates, only loss or damage *directly* resulting from the act of God is covered by this exemption; "consequential" (and therefore avoidable) loss and damage is not included.

Another aspect of this same question involves damage that takes place under act-of-God conditions (during flooding, severe storms, etc.) but involves defective carrier equipment—leaking highway trailers or rail cars, holes in tarpaulin covers, etc. It is established in law that the carrier is not exonerated from liability for the resulting damage in such circumstances.[6]

It is important that the act of God exception not be confused with the *force majeure* (also *vis major*) clause often found in contracts and excusing the parties for failing to meet the requirements of the contract if the failure was due to forces beyond their control. *Force majeure* is a much broader exclusion, encompassing not only what have been described above as acts of

---

[5] This case was never tried in court; after the author published his opinion on the legalities of the question in *Traffic World* magazine, the carrier paid the claim without further demur.

[6] *A., T. & S. F. Ry. Co. v. Eddie*, 61 Pac.2d 681.

EXCEPTIONS: 'ACT OF GOD'

God but also such other problems as labor strikes, riots, even mechanical breakdowns, and does not apply to the law of freight loss and damage.

7
The Exceptions (II): Act of a 'Public Enemy'

THE TERM "PUBLIC ENEMY," AS IT APPLIES INSOFAR AS CARRIERS are exculpated from liability for loss or damage resulting from the acts of such, includes only "the military forces of a nation at war with the domestic government."[1]

Only twice in the history of the United States as a nation—during the War of 1812, and then, of course, during the Civil War—has this country had to endure hostile military forces on its territory. This exception is therefore, realistically, fairly meaningless in terms of domestic surface transportation within the U.S.; and where foreign air or ocean carriage is involved, other legal principles peculiarly applicable to these modes broaden the scope of this exception considerably (*see below*).

In particular, the term "public enemy" does *not* embrace common criminals, even though they are sometimes referred to as such by law-enforcement agencies. Loss, damage or delay due to crime, no matter by whom committed, is *not* covered by one of the exceptions to the basic rule of carrier liability. This holds true even for acts of politically motivated sabotage, terrorism, etc.; in law these are not considered acts of a "public enemy," and the carrier is not excused from liability for injury to goods in its custody from such causes.

---

1   *Miller's Law of Freight Loss and Damage Claims*, 4th ed., by R. R. Sigmon (Dubuque, IA: Wm. C. Brown Publishers, 1974), pp. 92-93.

8
The Exceptions (III): Act of a 'Public Authority'

CARRIERS ARE NOT LIABLE FOR LOSS OR DAMAGE WHICH RESULTS from the act of some public (*i.e.*, governmental) authority, as when goods are seized or impounded by law-enforcement officials, Customs, etc.

"[The carrier] cannot be compelled to. . . accept all the consequences of resisting officers of the law. If he is excusable for yielding to a public enemy, he cannot be at fault for yielding to actual authority what he may yield to usurped authority."[1]

A particular problem in this regard can arise when (as has in the past occurred) law-enforcement officials recover goods stolen from a carrier, but impound them for use as evidence at the trial of the accused thief or thieves. In such circumstances the carrier is not liable for their "loss"—even though it may take months, even years, before the trial is completed and the goods released to their owner. On the other hand, as already noted, if the goods are *not* recovered the carrier *is* liable.

Also under this heading fall such things as seizure of contraband (drugs or other illicit substances) by police, reclamation of stolen articles, impoundment by Customs, condemnation by safety officials, confiscation of restricted farm produce by state or federal agricultural officials, delays due to legally required

---

1   *Pingree v. Railroad Co.*, 66 Mich. 143.

inspections, etc. However, it must again be emphasized that the act of a public authority, as with the other exceptions, must be the *sole* cause of the loss, damage or delay to exculpate the carrier.

9
The Exceptions (IV): Act of the Shipper

THE TERM "SHIPPER," INSOFAR AS THE LAW PROVIDES THAT THE carrier is not liable for loss, damage or delay result from the acts or omissions of such persons, is defined broadly enough to embrace consignor, consignee and anyone else who physically handles the freight in such capacities.

Most often this exception is invoked where there are alleged deficiencies in either (a) the loading of the goods by the consignor (or, less frequently, their unloading by the consignee), or (b) the packaging or other preparation of the goods for transportation. "The general rule is that, where the shipper packs articles for shipment, he cannot recover from the carrier for injuries due to improper packing"[1]—and that applies equally when the question is the propriety of the loading (stowage of the goods on board the carrier's vehicle or vessel).

There are, however, two important limitations to this exception. First, the loss or damage must have resulted *solely* from the improper loading or packaging. Even if the shipper loaded or packaged the goods inadequately, the carrier is still liable if there were also some other, non-excepted cause that contributed to the injury.

Especially where loading or packaging is marginal—ade-

---

1 *Northwestern Marble & Tile Co. v. Williams*, 151 N.W. 419.

quate, perhaps, for a "soft" trip but not a "hard" one—this can give rise to disputes between shippers and carriers, with legal decisions turning on the tiniest of details of the actual journey. The following case, which aroused considerable controversy when the author published his opinion on it in a trade publication,[2] illustrates the type of problem that can arise:

An extremely large and heavy (60,000 pounds) print roller, used in newspaper printing presses, was shipped by truck to a repair facility. It was set in a wooden cradle, and encased by two-inch-thick crating. This initial journey was without incident, and so, after the repairs had been made, was most of the return trip—until, a very short distance from the ultimate destination, the driver was obliged by traffic conditions to make an emergency "panic stop." The roller crashed through the front of the crating and was seriously damaged.

The author gave his opinion (which he still believes to be correct; the case was never litigated in court) that the damage was ascribable to inadequate packaging, and that the carrier was therefore not liable for the damage. There was no evidence to refute the truck driver's claim that (a) he had been driving safely, prudently and within the speed limit, and (b) he could not have reasonably foreseen the need for an abrupt stop, which arose when a car emerged from a side street directly in front of him. Since it appeared that this sudden stop, alone, had led directly to the damage, the author took this as *prima facie* (at first glance) evidence that the crating—although adequate for most purposes—was not sufficient to withstand the effects of hard vehicle braking; and since such braking is an ordinary and foreseeable

---

[2] The "Questions and Answers" column of *Traffic World* magazine; for those who wish to pursue this case in greater detail, the discussions were reprinted in hardcover in *Traffic World's Questions & Answers*, Vol. 29, p. 179 *et seq.* (Washington, DC: International Thomson Transport Press, 1985).

hazard of highway transportation, the author's view was that this rendered the packaging inadequate.

It's important to note that others, including one well-known authority in the field of loss-and-damage liability law, expressed strong disagreement with the author's view. And certainly there is room for such a difference of opinion in the circumstances described, where the cargo is adequately packed for normal but not for abnormal (albeit not unforeseeable) conditions of transportation. The effects of badly maintained roads, "humping" of railroad cars, etc., not infrequently give rise to similar disputes, the resolution of which is not at all clear-cut.

Carriers have attempted to minimize such controversies by publishing, in tariff form, detailed guides to how particular types of goods should be packaged.[3] Since tariff guidelines are often (not surprisingly) quite stringent, and complying with them fully can be fairly expensive, many shippers use alternate forms of packaging; but if the guidelines are not followed, carriers are prone to treat virtually *all* loss and damage as having been caused by inadequate packaging. However, the law does not support such an indiscriminate approach; although failure to observe tariff-published packaging standards is certainly a strike against the shipper, it does not, alone, prove that either (a) the packaging was necessarily inadequate, or (b) the loss or damage was the proximate result of the packaging deficiency.

The carrier must also have been unaware of the adequacies in loading and/or packaging when it received the shipment at origin in order to successfully claim this exception.

"Where a shipper tenders to a carrier goods for transportation which are insufficiently crated, boxed, packed or loaded, *and such insufficiency is discoverable by the carrier upon ordinary observation and inspection*, it is the duty of the carrier to refuse to receive the goods," one court put it. ". . . [I]f the

---

3 See esp. the National Motor Freight Classification.

carrier does accept the goods, it may not thereafter allege that any injury which they sustained in the course of transportation was due to such insufficient crating, boxing, packing or loading."[4]

Note that, in the foregoing, the court says it is enough if the carrier *should have known* of the loading or packaging deficiency (that the defect was "discoverable. . . upon ordinary observation and inspection") not that it necessarily *did* know. Although this particular proviso of the law is rarely invoked, it can be of significance in some circumstances, such as where repetitive shipments of the same commodity, packed and loaded in the same way, are made with recurrent loss-and-damage problems.

Especially in these days of intense marketplace competition among transportation carriers, this can produce some awkward real-world results. It is all very well for the courts to tell carriers they must either refuse an inadequately packaged or loaded shipment altogether or accept liability for any loss or damage due to packaging or loading problems. But what is the carrier to do when one of its biggest shippers tells it, in effect, "Accept this shipment or we'll stop giving you *any* freight"?

No past cases deal with this very significant issue of coercion, and it remains a clouded area. The opinion of the author, however, is that solid evidence of such coercion on the shipper's part might well suffice to overcome the foreknowledge limitation of the inadequate-packaging defense. It seems improbable that a court would uphold the claim of a shipper who not only ignored warnings that his packaging was inadequate but made threats to the carrier who gave them in order to compel that carrier to haul the freight "as is."

It should also be noted that inadequacy in both packaging and, especially, loading may have consequences far beyond loss

---

4   *Thompson v. C., M. & St. P. Ry. Co.*, 217 N.W. 927; emphasis added.

of or damage to the mispackaged/misloaded freight itself. Both shippers and carriers may expose themselves to potentially catastrophic liability should packaging or loading defects result in safety problems. Cases of this nature that have come to the author's personal attention have involved improper loading or bracing that caused the cargo to shift suddenly in transit, resulting in train derailments or highway accidents.

In this context it is worth noting that carriers may be held liable for the consequences of such mishaps—personal injury or loss of life as well as property damage or destruction—and that, if the shipper actually performed the loading or its mispackaging led or contributed to the problem, it, too, may be obliged in law to share in such liability.[5] In addition, of course, failure to package or load properly for transportation may subject carriers, and possibly shippers, to fines or civil forfeitures for causing safety hazards.

Occasionally mis-marking of packages—especially on less-than-truckload motor carrier shipments, where the goods must be transloaded by the carrier—will result in invocation of the act-of-the-shipper defense. Clearly the carrier cannot be held liable for misdelivering or otherwise misplacing goods that are not properly marked with the consignee's name and address, nor for failing to use special care in the handling of commodities where the requirements—"Fragile", "This Side Up", etc.—are not made known to the carrier through appropriate markings.

One such problem that was brought to the author's attention involved a 2'x2'x9' crate that, at the time the motor carrier arrived to pick it up, was standing upright on a pallet. The

---

5   The shipper is held in law to give the carrier an "implied warranty" that his shipment is packaged, loaded (if he does the loading), etc., in a manner suitable for safe transportation. If it develops that this is not the case, even though the shipper may not have been aware of the defect, he is responsible for any resulting injury or damage. *Eastern Motor Exp., Inc. v. Maschmeijer, Jr., Inc.*, 247 F.2d 826, reversing 141 F.Supp. 477, cert. den. 355 U.S. 959.

carrier's van could not accommodate this height (nine feet plus the pallet depth), and the driver asked the shipper if the crate might be laid on its side. The shipper agreed, and the crate was laid down on the pallet; however, in this position it overhung the edges of the pallet by a considerable margin, which placed excessive torque stress on the goods inside the crate and resulted in damage. The carrier could not be held liable, of course, since the shipper had agreed to the shipping position of the crate and the carrier had no way of knowing that this position was inappropriate.

However, mis-marking (or failure to mark), and/or misstatements on the bill of lading or other shipping documents, will serve to excuse the carrier from liability only if these faults are (1) directly and (2) solely responsible for the loss or damage. Otherwise, mis-marking, misdescription, etc., on either the packages or the shipping documents does not affect the carrier's liability.[6]

Another especially contention-rife area in which the act-of-the-shipper exemption is often invoked by carriers is in conjunction with so-called "shipper's load and count" shipments. Curiously, this is one of the most poorly understood areas of freight loss and damage law notwithstanding that it (unlike most other principles of the law, which rely mainly on past court decisions) is spelled out quite clearly in the statute itself.

"[W]hen package freight or bulk freight is loaded by a shipper and the goods are described in a bill of lading merely by a statement of marks or labels. . ., or by a statement that the goods are said to be. . . of a certain kind or quantity, or in a certain condition, or it is stated in the bill of lading that packages

---

6 If, however, the shipper *intentionally* misdescribed the goods for fraudulent purposes (such as to secure the benefit of lower rates), the carrier is relieved from liability as a carrier, although court decisions are divided as to whether it remains liable as an ordinary bailee (warehouseman) or has no liability at all. See *Corpus Juris Secundum*, 13 C.J.S. Carriers § 78(b).

are said to contain goods of a certain kind or quantity or in a certain condition, or that the contents or condition of the contents of packages are unknown, or words of like purport are contained in the bill of lading, . . . such statements, if true, shall not make liable the carrier issuing the bill of lading, although the goods are not of the kind or quantity or in the condition they were said to be by the consignor. . . .

"The carrier may also, by inserting in the bill of lading the words 'Shipper's weight, load and count,' or other words of like purport, indicate that the goods were loaded by the shipper and the description of them made by him; and if such statement be true, the carrier shall not be liable for damages caused by the improper loading or by the nonreceipt or by the misdescription of the goods described in the bill of lading. . . ."[7]

Thus, if the shipper (a) physically loads the goods, and (b) inadvertently misrepresents them on the shipping documents, the carrier is not liable for any shortages, damage, etc., that appear to have occurred based on the incorrect B/L description. The law allows the carrier to identify shipments as having been shipper-loaded (the common commercial terminology is "Shipper's Load & Count") in order to facilitate its handling of claims, but this provision is permissive only; if the shipper actually *did* do the loading, the same principle governs even if the SL&C notation was omitted.

And that holds true in reverse, too:

". . . [W]hen goods are loaded by a carrier, such carrier shall count the packages of goods, if package freight, and ascertain the kind and quantity, if bulk freight, and such carrier shall not, in such cases, insert in the bill of lading or in any notice, receipt, contract, rule, regulation or tariff, 'Shipper's weight, load and count,' or other words of like purport. . . . If

---

7   Pomerene (Bills of Lading) Act, 21 (49 U.S.C. § 101).

so inserted [in the bill of lading or other shipment documentation] contrary to the provisions of this section, such words shall be treated as null and void and as if not inserted therein."[8]

In other words, it's the *facts*, not the B/L notation (or absence thereof), that govern. And the entire thrust of all this statutory language is merely to exonerate the carrier, under the act-of-the-shipper doctrine, from having to assume liability for loading problems, errors in counting, etc., made by the shipper. Nothing could be more straightforward, it would appear.

Yet over the decades the "Shipper's Load & Count" notation has become invested with a mystique that's only loosely (at best) related to this statutory language. Carriers not infrequently seek to disavow virtually *all* liability for shipments moving on B/L's that bear this notation, whether or not the loss or damage has anything to do with the loading or counting of the goods. They will routinely reject claims on such shipments no matter how much evidence the shipper provides of the count or condition of the load at origin, notwithstanding that the statute, in perhaps the most explicit language to be found in any area of L&D liability law, does not countenance or support such an attitude.

And shippers, perhaps in reaction, have adopted the general practice of resisting such B/L notations as vigorously as they can. Some shippers, for example, seek to require that the representatives of motor carriers serving them remain at or near the loading gate to "observe" the loading and, presumably, verify the count, and on that basis disallow the SL&C notation. That one driver with two eyes cannot possibly observe completely and accurately the activities of a full loading crew, perhaps assisted by power equipment, is to them irrelevant; but it will emphatically *not* be irrelevant to any court considering a loss-and-damage lawsuit.

A related sort of controversy arises with some frequency

---

8 *Ibid.*, § 20 (49 U.S.C. § 100).

EXCEPTIONS: ACT OF THE SHIPPER

when packaged goods are handled on pallets, skids, slipsheets or in otherwise unitized fashion. Many carriers will issue bills of lading showing only the number of such pallets or other shipping units, rather than the piece count of the individual packages, and will automatically reject claims for shortage if the proper number of pallets or units was delivered.

If the carrier cannot physically count the packages loaded on a pallet because of nesting, etc.—or because the driver lacks the time to make a full piece count during palletized loading—its reluctance to swear that it indeed received a given number of packages for transportation is understandable. There may well be internal, invisible voids in the apparently solid stack of cartons, or the stacking pattern may be optically deceptive, etc. But refusal to identify the stated (by the shipper) number of packages on the bill of lading is a somewhat dubious means of resolving this dilemma; and many carriers have shifted to variants on the SL&C notation instead.

In any event, the carrier can scarcely disclaim liability for any packages that provably disappeared in transit on this ground. To suggest, as some carriers do, that they are responsible only for delivering the proper number of pallets or other aggregated shipping units, irrespective of whether packages stacked on those pallets/units have or have not vanished, is puerile; it makes no more sense than for the carrier to contend that it has discharged its responsibility to deliver a load of packaged freight by delivering only empty cartons. As with shipper's load and count, it is the facts, as proved by substantive evidence, that must govern in such cases.

Concealed loss and damage claims also are (at least in law) controlled by the same standard. Indeed, such claims constitute simply another variant on the shipper's load and count and palletized-load problems, and represent in fact the generic case within the context of which both of these are merely subdivisions. Unfortunately, albeit understandably, these claims, too, often become fraught with controversy.

"Understandably" because, by the nature of its being concealed, such loss or damage cannot be observed to have occurred at any particular time (or, more importantly, while the goods were in any party's physical custody). It may reasonably be considered—although even this may be open to question in particular cases—that the goods were intact and complete at the time they were enclosed in packaging; and likewise (and with the same *caveat*) it may be considered that they were damaged, or in part or in whole missing, when they were removed from that packaging.

In between, however, they passed through the hands of *at least* three parties—those of the shipper prior to delivery to the carrier for transportation, those of the carrier, and those of the consignee following delivery. And where did the loss or damage actually occur in this chain of events?

On various occasions carriers have sought to establish, by publication in regulatory tariffs or deregulated rate circulars, absolutist standards for pro-rating such claims. Typically, such standards have sought to assign liability on the basis of the goods' "exposure" to loss or damage, with each transfer of possession from one party to another being treated as one such "exposure." Thus, in the simplest case, a concealed damage claim would be regarded as having had three "exposures"—while in the custody of the shipper, while the carrier had it, and after delivery to the consignee—and the carrier would be liable for one-third of the amount of the damage.

When such provisions have come up for adjudication before the Interstate Commerce Commission that agency has, quite properly (as a legal matter), disallowed them. Under the law the carrier is or is not liable, based on the facts of each individual case; *pro rata* settlements of claims, although acceptable if the parties agree in a particular case, may not be imposed by tariff or other rule by one party on another.

Thus, each case must hinge, in law, on the quantity and quality of the evidence the parties may offer. In some cases the facts will be such as to provide at least inferential proof that the loss or damage took place while the goods were in the custody of one or another of the parties; in others there will be no such inference available, and resolution must depend on the unsupported testimony of individual witnesses.

In many instances carriers seek to fix a time limit, usually quite brief,[9] for the filing of concealed damage claims; claims filed after expiration of the specified time, they state, will be automatically disallowed. Such time limits have no validity in law; they are merely, *de facto*, policy statements by carrier managements concerning their intention of contesting claims. In effect, the carrier is saying it will at least consider claims filed within the time limit without requiring full proof that the concealed loss or damage took place while the goods were in its (the carrier's) custody, but will defend all claims filed after the specified time has passed. But if the shipper has adequate evidence to support its claim, the law gives little or no weight to such time limits.

---

9   The best-known of these is the 15-day time limit specified in the National Motor Freight Classification.

10
The Exceptions (V): 'Inherent Vice'

"INHERENT VICE" TRANSLATES TO MEAN THE PECULIAR CHARACteristics or nature of the goods themselves which may render the loss or damage unavoidable.

". . . [T]he carrier is not liable for loss or injury due solely to such causes as fermentation, depreciation, drying, decay, heating merely as a result of transportation, spontaneous combustion, effervescence, putrefaction, or corrosion or rusting resulting from the chemical union of parts of the goods shipped," says one widely respected legal compendium. ". . . [I]t may be stated as a general proposition that the carrier is not liable for loss happening through the operation of natural causes without negligence or fault of the carrier."[1]

This exception is most commonly applied to perishable foodstuffs, drugs, etc., which, although transported promptly by the carrier under the conditions specified by the shipper, may nevertheless have spoiled en route. However, there are other occasions where the defense may also be invoked. Steel, for example, may rust if exposed to moisture. Some non-perishables are vulnerable to injury due to temperature extremes. And so forth.

In some instances precautions may be taken against the possibility of such injury, such as (most commonly) protecting

---
1 *Corpus Juris Secundum*, 13 C.J.S. Carriers § 79.

them from extremes of heat and/or cold. If such protection is essential, however, it is up to the shipper to specify it in the shipping instructions he gives to the carrier; and failure to do so is apt to be fatal to his claim should damage result from such causes.[2] However, the inherent vice defense will not serve to exculpate the carrier from the consequences of its failure to live up to commitments implicit in its undertaking to haul the freight by virtue of, for example, the equipment used. For example, highway "dry vans," railroad boxcars, etc., are expected to be proof against ordinary precipitation; if goods experience water damage due to leaky equipment, the carrier may not be heard to argue that—since not all types of goods would be damaged by water—the susceptibility of these particular goods to such damage constitutes inherent vice within the meaning of this exclusion.

The question of inherent vice frequently arises in claims arising from contamination or infestation of goods. Contamination is, of course, adulteration of goods (generally, though not always, commodities shipped in bulk) by some other incompatible substance—salt in the sugar and so forth. Infestation is likewise the adulteration of goods, but by living creatures—insects, vermin, etc. Both can result in significant problems, especially in circumstances where purity requirements are high, as with foodstuffs and certain industrial chemicals and other substances.

An entertaining, if largely irrelevant, example of the stringency of purity requirements in some cases was provided the

---

[2] In this context it should be noted that it may *not* be enough that goods are not susceptible to damage from reasonably expectable ambient air temperatures, especially where excess heat is concerned. The temperature inside a closed highway van or rail car may easily reach 160° Fahrenheit or more in an ordinary sunny summer day, notwithstanding that the thermometer outdoors reads sixty or eighty degrees lower. A good rule of thumb is for the shipper to ask for temperature protection for any goods vulnerable to heat injury at anything very much below 180° or so (although experience will of course be the best guide).

EXCEPTIONS: 'INHERENT VICE'

author by an individual whose company dealt with turbine oil, which must be entirely contaminant-free to avoid damage to the machinery in which it is used. All incoming loads of the product are spot-checked for impurities before being discharged from the bulk transportation equipment, and in the instance in question the oil was found to be contaminated by dirt in the trailer.

The carrier returned the load for reprocessing (at its expense) and had the trailer chemically cleaned. The oil was re-delivered, and again found to be contaminated, this time by the cleaning compounds. Once again it was reprocessed and the trailer was re-cleaned; this time the carrier's manager instructed one of his employees to manually scrub down the interior of the tank to remove any chemical residue. On redelivery, however, the oil was *again* found to be contaminated, by fibers from the clothing of the individual who scrubbed the trailer.

In exasperation the manager ordered the trailer re-cleaned and again manually scrubbed; but this time he directed his employee to strip naked before climbing inside the trailer. The again-reprocessed oil was delivered, but was once more rejected —for contamination by human hair!

In cases of claimed contamination or infestation, a determination must be made as to whether the problem arose while the goods were in transit. If so, the carrier may generally not invoke the inherent vice defense; it won't be heard to argue that, for example, it's not liable for infestation of a load of candy by ants because the candy's nature is such that it attracts ants—provided that the ants got into the load while it was in the carrier's custody. On the other hand, if the ants were already present at the time the goods were loaded the carrier is excused.

This principle is also extended to problems that arise in transit, resulting in loss or damage, out of *root causes* that were present at the time the goods were tendered to the carrier. In one instance, a carrier was excused from liability for fire damage to a load of cotton when the court found that smoldering embers were embedded in a bale at the time the cotton was loaded.[3] Another situation that came to the author's attention (although it never reached litigation) involved a load of clothing damaged by moths; evidence showed that when the clothing was loaded it was infested with larvae, which evolved into mature moths while the goods were in transit.

Once again, the inherent vice of the freight must be the *sole* cause of the injury in order to excuse the carrier. Deterioration of fresh produce when transit has been delayed (without regard to whether the carrier was or was not at fault for the delay), for instance, will not be ascribed to inherent vice for purposes of excusing the carrier, since the delay, too, was a contributory factor.

---

[3] *Gulf, C. & S. F. Ry. Co. v. Downs*, 70 S.W.2d 318.

11
The Exceptions: The 'But-For' Rule

AS SOME OF THE FOREGOING DISCUSSION INDICATES, THE ENUmerated exceptions will only serve to exonerate the carrier from liability for loss, damage or delay if the named causes are (a) directly and (b) completely (100%) responsible.

This is sometimes referred to as the "but-for" rule; that is, the goods must have been secure *but for* intervention of the excepted cause. If some other non-excepted cause played any part at all in the sequence of events that led to the loss, damage or delay, the carrier is entirely liable just as if the excepted cause(s) was (were) not involved at all.

In particular, the carrier may not have contributed in any way to the problem by its own negligence (or that of its employees, agents, etc.). Any "contributory negligence" whatsoever on the carrier's part subjects it to liability for the entire economic injury.

It must be emphasized that this concept of "contributory negligence" does *not* cut both ways; that is, the carrier may not plead negligence by the shipper (or anyone else) if that only contributed to, but was not the sole cause of, the loss, damage or delay. One court discussed this question in the following terms:

"It appears to us that the rules of contributory negligence have no application in [a freight loss and damage] case. Contributory negligence of plaintiff is a defense only in cases where the action is founded on negligence of defendant. . . . The carrier's common law liability is founded, not on negligence, but 'on broad principles of public policy and convenience, and was introduced to prevent the necessity of going into circumstances impossible to be unraveled.'"[1]

The shipper's error, thus, may have been 99% responsible for the problem; but if even 1% of the fault lay elsewhere, the carrier is fully liable. This is the main "inequity" identified by the ICC in its Staggers Act study of the regime of carrier liability (*see above*), but has become so entrenched in transportation practices and economics that the Commission recommended no change even in this particular.

It's important to recognize that the same holds true whether if the contributory cause was *not* the carrier's negligence or some other event, possibly even entirely beyond the carrier's control, which is, however, not covered by one of the five named exceptions. This is the meaning and purport of the carrier's status as "virtual insuror" of the goods; unless the *entire* loss, damage or delay resulted from a provable excepted cause, the carrier is responsible without regard to whatever role the excepted cause may have played.

Finally, it may be that the loss, damage or delay came about in two separate increments—one due to an excepted cause, and the other not, as with the illustrative discussion of a lightning-caused fire and subsequent rain damage when goods were left outdoors after being removed from the building (*above*). In such a case, provided the two occurrences can be clearly distinguished, the carrier won't be liable for any economic loss resulting from the one, but *is* liable with respect to the other.

---

[1] *Northwestern Marble and Tile Co. v. Williams*, 151 N.W. 419.

12
The Role of Negligence

AS ALREADY DISCUSSED, NEGLIGENCE BY THE CARRIER WILL render it liable for loss of, damage to or delay of goods in its custody notwithstanding any role that may have been played by one or more of the enumerated excepted causes.

The term "negligence," although often used in casual conversation to encompass a wide range of behaviors, has, in law, a more specific meaning. "Negligence," said one of the British courts that first wrestled with its definition, "is the omission to do something which a reasonable man, guided upon those considerations which ordinarily regulate the conduct of human affairs, would do, or doing something which a prudent and reasonable man would not do."[1]

In reality, of course, there is no such person as this apocryphal "prudent and reasonable man"; he is a figment of the judicial imagination, invoked as a measure of human conduct. Thus, the precise definition of what such an individual would or would not do will vary somewhat heuristically, depending in some degree on the particular judge or jury that is doing the imagining. To be sure, there is a vast body of legal precedent to fix parameters for what is prudent and reasonable and what isn't; but since the range of possible behavior and situations is virtually infinite, it's not unusual to encounter circumstances for which the body of the law fixes no exact guidelines. In sum,

---

1 *Blyth v. Birmingham Waterworks Co.*, 11 Ex. 781, 784, 156 Eng.Rep. 1047.

negligence must in the final analysis be defined based on the facts and circumstances of each case, and cannot be generically specified with any precision.

The result of this uncertainty is to place a significant burden on the party obliged to submit legal proof on the negligence issue. In most areas of the law of bailments that party is the claimant; he must affirmatively demonstrate negligence on the defendant's part in order to recover damages. The law of transportation carrier liability, however, inverts this situation, establishing a presumption that the carrier *was* negligent and requiring it to prove otherwise.

In a popular child's fairy tale an elf promises to grant untold riches to anyone who can sit for half an hour and consciously *not* think of the word "hippopotamus." In a sense this is the conundrum confronted by the carrier on the negligence issue; it is obviously much easier to single out a particular action and demonstrate that *it* was (or wasn't) negligent than to examine the entire *gestalt* of behavior over a span of perhaps several days and demonstrate that *none* of it may be so considered. The courts have broadly adopted an evidentiary approach that makes the carrier's burden of proof a feasible one (*see below*), but it remains substantial.

And if the carrier fails to show its non-negligence, its status as "virtual insuror" of the goods remains unchallenged, and it is liable for the loss/damage/delay being claimed against it.

Negligence may be an issue in connection with misrouting or misdelivery of shipments by the carrier. The author was told of one case in which a shipment of goods subject to damage if frozen was shipped without any requirements for protective service by the carrier. The shipment originated at and was destined to sun-belt points, so that freezing was not expected to be a problem. However, the carrier erroneously loaded the shipment aboard a vehicle that traveled far north of the normal route; ambient temperatures dipped well below freezing, and the goods were damaged. Since the misrouting was due to the carrier's

THE ROLE OF NEGLIGENCE

negligence, it was liable notwithstanding that it had no means of knowing that the goods were susceptible to such damage.

Strictly speaking, problems involving misdelivery do not fall under the heading of "loss or damage"; as a legal matter they constitute "conversion" by the carrier.[2] Since the law treats conversion on the same plane as loss or damage, however, this is a distinction without a difference; handling of claims and/or lawsuits is the same.

Misdelivery of goods—that is, delivery to someone other than the designated consignee—is a form of conversion for which the carrier is liable just as it would be if they had been lost or damaged. But its liability is contingent on the misdelivery having resulted from its own negligence; if the misdelivery resulted from some other cause, such as misidentification of the consignee by the shipper, the carrier is not liable.

An interesting variation on this general theme arose in a case the author encountered. The carrier made delivery of the goods to the proper consignee's shipping dock, where they were received by an individual representing himself to be an employee of the consignee; but in fact, it developed, he was an interloper who promptly absconded with the freight. In such circumstances, of course, the carrier could scarcely be held liable, since it had in no way been negligent. However, where goods are held on the carrier's premises for customer pickup, the carrier has an affirmative duty to verify the identity of the person making the pickup, and its failure to do so will render it liable if that person

---

2   "Conversion" is the shorthand way the law refers to one party converting the goods or chattels of another to its own use, and is used in reference to circumstances in which a bailee having possession of goods for a particular purpose goes beyond that purpose in its handling of the goods—that is, does something with the goods which was not commanded or authorized by their owner. If, and to the extent that, this results in an injury to the goods' owner, the party guilty of conversion is liable for the economic consequences of that injury.

proves not to have been authorized by the consignee to make the pickup.[3]

Even delivery to the *proper* consignee may subject the carrier to liability if it ignores post-shipment instructions by the shipper not to make such delivery. For instance, the shipper may discover, after the goods are dispatched but before they are delivered, that the consignee is insolvent, and seek to exercise its right of stoppage *in transitu*. If the stop order is issued in time for the carrier to act on it, the carrier's non-compliance will render it liable should the consignee fail to pay the shipper's invoice.

(Obviously this gives rise to potential problems, should the shipper instruct that the goods be held up at the same time the consignee is insisting that delivery be made. The carrier should not allow itself to be thus put in the middle of a dispute between shipper and consignee, and is justified in refusing to turn the goods over to *anyone* until and unless it is provided with clear proof of title.)

In general, negligence *as a legal question* arises in connection with loss-and-damage claims much less frequently than one might suppose from reviewing carrier and shipper claim files. Those files commonly reflect a widespread misunderstanding of the underlying law, which often results in disputes between the parties that are entirely misdirected.

Such disputes typically commence with the claimant accusing the carrier—either in the claim itself or in associated correspondence—of "negligence" in its handling of the lost/ damaged/ delayed freight. It may be that the claimant's managerial personnel are under the mistaken impression that negligence by the carrier is a necessary precondition to recovery on the claim; or the word may be used (out of anger or frustration) in its connotative sense of implying misbehavior or carelessness on the carrier's part.

These same considerations (especially the latter) are likely

---

3   *Corpus Juris Secundum*, 13 C.J.S. Carriers § 174(b).

THE ROLE OF NEGLIGENCE

to prompt the carrier to respond in kind, indignantly denying any negligence and perhaps even seeking to mirror the accusation back at the shipper. And in short order discussions about the claim have deteriorated into a profitless dispute over who was negligent and who was not, and to what extent, etc., notwithstanding that the issue may well not even be relevant to the validity of the claim.

Under the law, the question of negligence *does not even arise* unless the carrier can *successfully* assert one of the five exculpatory defenses. That is, the carrier's own behavior may have been blameless, even praiseworthy; but it remains liable for the economic consequences unless it can demonstrate that the loss, damage or delay resulted necessarily and inevitably from one or another of these five causes.

Only if it can so demonstrate does its own behavior come under scrutiny. Did it contribute to the problem, either through its actions or its failure to act? In some instances the question of negligence will still not arise, if the carrier can prove that the answer to both parts of this question is in the negative. Only if what the carrier did—or what it might have done but didn't—played a role in the real-world scenario will the "prudence and reasonableness" of what it did or didn't do (*i.e.*, its negligence or non-negligence) become of legal consequence.

This point cannot be overemphasized: *Negligence is not a necessary precondition to a finding of common carrier liability.* The carrier may have been victimized by forces entirely outside its control—may have been robbed by Lord Holt's hypothetical "irresistible multitude of people"—and still be legally liable for the shipper's economic loss. Especially since accusations of negligence carry a considerable emotional "charge," arousing antagonisms at a level where they are hard to dissipate, it will ordinarily be advisable to avoid them unless the question is legally in issue with regard to a particular claim.

13
Regulated v. Unregulated Carriage

IT IS IMPORTANT TO RECOGNIZE THAT THE LIABILITY REGIME described above applies to all domestic overland carriers—railroads, motor carriers and freight forwarders employing the services of these modes (*although see below*)—without regard to their regulatory status. The legal principles outlined are founded in the so-called common law—*i.e.*, the body of law comprised of precedent decisions of the courts—and are hence applicable to all such common carriers whether or not subject to such specific statutes as the Interstate Commerce Act.

However, there are two provisions incorporated in the so-called Carmack Amendment to the IC Act[1] which are not to be found in the common law, and which accordingly have application only to the extent that the carriage is subject to economic regulatory jurisdiction.

The first and most important of these is the concept of "joint and several liability" by carriers participating in through interline movements. Ordinarily a carrier will be liable only for such loss of, damage to or delay of goods as occurs when the goods are in its custody. Especially with regard to concealed or inconspicuous loss or damage, this may present a problem to the claimant where the goods have been handled by two or more carriers in

---

1 Incorporated in the present statute as 49 U.S.C. § 11707.

the course of their origin-to-destination movement; without evidence as to which carrier had possession of the goods at the time of the loss or damage, the claimant will be unable to recover from any of them.

The concept of joint and several liability resolves this dilemma by treating all carriers participating in a through interline movement as *de facto* partners for the purpose of that movement. Just as all partners are liable, individually and collectively, for the acts or failings of the partnership, so do all the interlining carriers involved in the move share loss and damage liability without regard to which of them may have had the goods in its possession at the time of the loss or damage.

Under the IC Act, claim for loss or damage on an interlined shipment may be filed against either the originating carrier or the carrier making final delivery; and if *any* participating carrier is shown to be liable, the claim must be paid.[2]

Note that claims should generally not be filed against "bridge" carriers—those which neither originated nor delivered the shipment, but merely handled it between intermediate points. A claim filed with such a bridge carrier will be valid only to the extent that the loss/damage/delay took place while the goods were in that carrier's hands; but joint and several liability is not invoked by the filing of a claim with a bridge carrier.

In addition, with respect to railroads, the law specifies that the "delivering" carrier is considered to be the last carrier that performed *line-haul* transportation of the shipment; that is, carriers performing only a switching service at destination are not deemed to be "delivering" carriers.

However, in cases of non-delivery of any portion of the

---

2 Carriers ordinarily apportion such losses among themselves, according to their individual liability, by means of interline claims. However, such apportionment need, in law, be of no concern to the claimant; and payment to the claimant may not legally be delayed or withheld pending resolution of interline claims problems or questions.

shipment there will, of course, be no "delivering" carrier; that is, claim may *not* be filed with the carrier that would ordinarily have handled delivery by virtue of routing instructions on the bill of lading, interline arrangements among carriers, etc. In such cases claim must be filed with either the origin carrier or the last carrier in the routing to have had physical custody of the freight.

It is interesting to note that, in Great Britain, developments in the common law during the 19th century have assigned joint and several liability to all carriers participating in interline service. In the United States, however, the common law does not include such a provision; joint and several liability in this country is assigned only by the IC Act, and is therefore only applicable to the extent that service is subject to its jurisdiction—*i.e.*, is economically regulated.

The second distinction between the common law and the IC Act lies in the time allowed for filing claims and lawsuits. The Act specifies that transportation contracts may allow no less than nine months from the date of delivery (or, in the case of undelivered shipments, the date on which delivery would ordinarily have been made) for the filing of claims, and no less than two years and a day from the carrier's declination of a claim for the filing of lawsuits.[3] Where service is not subject to IC Act jurisdiction, these constraints don't apply.

With respect to motor carriage, the jurisdiction of these two

---

3   From a legal point of view it's important to recognize that these limits are *not* "statutes of limitation." A statute of limitation fixes a set time limit for the taking of some action, which (depending on the statute) may or may not be alterable by agreement of the parties. With regard to the periods for the filing of L&D claims and lawsuits, by contrast, the law expressly states that these time limits are to be fixed by contract (*i.e.*, the bill of lading), but disallows any contractual limitations less than the prescribed minima. The parties may, thus, agree to *longer* than nine months for the filing of claims and two years and a day for the filing of lawsuits (although rarely, if ever, is this done), but any agreement purporting to establish a *shorter* time will be disallowed as contrary to law.

provisions of the Carmack Amendment largely parallels the economic regulatory jurisdiction of the Interstate Commerce Commission. Major exemptions from ICC regulation of motor freight transportation are:

(1) Intrastate transportation—that is, transportation taking place entirely within the borders, and over the roads, of a single state.[4]

(2) Transportation between contiguous municipalities (cities or towns having a common border) or within "commercial zones" (suburban, industrial, etc., areas surrounding an incorporated municipality).

(3) Transportation wholly within national parks or national monuments.

(4) Certain service performed for non-members by agricultural cooperative associations, within prescribed limitations.

(5) Certain transportation by owner-operators in backhaul service involving fronthaul transportation of agricultural commodities, again within prescribed limitations.

(6) Pickup and delivery service performed in conjunction with, or line-haul service performed in "occasional" substitution for, air transportation service (as to which liability is subject to the regime applicable to air carriage—*see below*).

(7) "Compensated intercorporate hauling"—*i.e.*, transportation by one 100% affiliated member of a corporate family on behalf of another 100% affiliate.

(8) Newspaper distribution service.

(9) Transportation of certain specific commodities and commodity groups:

    (a) Livestock.

    (b) Agricultural and horticultural commodities.

    (c) Various unprocessed or slightly processed foodstuffs identified by the ICC.

---

4   The regulatory laws of some—but not all—states extend such joint and several liability to and establish minimum claim-filing periods for motor carriers operating in regulated intrastate service.

REGULATED V. UNREGULATED CARRIAGE

(d) Livestock and poultry feed, and agricultural seeds and plants, when moving to and from farms and/or farm supply businesses.

(e) Fish and shellfish, cooked or uncooked (but not treated for preserving other than by freezing), and fish and shellfish by-products.

(f) Used empty shipping containers, except such containers employed in the transportation of automotive vehicles and parts.

(g) Decorative stone.

(h) Wood chips.[5]

Application of the Carmack Amendment to rail service, on the other hand, is not merely coextensive with ICC economic regulation. The Staggers Rail Act empowered the Commission to administratively exempt any rail service as to which it deemed regulation was unnecessary, an authority it has exercised to exempt (as of this writing) rail transportation of agricultural produce, much (although not all) boxcar service, transportation in refrigerated ("reefer") equipment, trailer-on-flat-car (TOFC or "piggyback") service, etc.

However, the statute further provides that "[n]o exemption order. . . shall. . . relieve any rail carrier from an obligation to provide contractual terms for liability and claims which are consistent with the provisions of [the Carmack Amendment]. . . ."[6] Although railroads are permitted to offer, on such deregulated service, "alternative terms" of liability,[7] they must maintain a "basic" level of service based on all Carmack-required liability standards, including joint and several liability and the claims and lawsuit time limits.

As of this writing, the ICC was also considering the extent to which it might administratively deregulate the motor carrier portion of rail TOFC movements, as well, under this provision

---

5 See 49 U.S.C. § 10526.
6 49 U.S.C. § 10505(e).
7 *Ibid.*

of the law. To the extent such service is deregulated, it, too, would be subject to the same restriction concerning Carmack applicability.

In addition, although intrastate railroad service is exempt from Federal regulation *per se*, the Staggers Act[8] expressly provides for the various states to employ identical standards in their own regulation of rail service, and further provides for the ICC to assert supervening jurisdiction over intrastate rail service in states that decline to do so. Accordingly, the Carmack Amendment's liability regime extends over intrastate rail operations as well.

---

8 49 U.S.C. § 11501.

14
Waterborne Transportation

LIABILITY FOR LOSS AND DAMAGE TO CARGO TRANSPORTED BY an ocean common carrier in the U.S. foreign trade (*i.e.*, generally between a U.S. ocean port and an ocean port in a foreign country[1]) is governed by the 1936 Carriage of Goods by Sea Act (COGSA).[2]

COGSA derives from, and in essence represents a codification of, the International Convention for the Unification of Certain Rules Relating to Bills of Lading 1924, an instrument commonly referred to as the Hague Rules. Virtually all seafaring nations are signatories to the Hague Rules, which are thus widely applicable to all ocean commerce (although this isn't invariably the case—*see below*).

There are two basic exceptions to the COGSA regime: (1) Transportation of livestock, and (2) cargo carried on deck in specific accordance with the terms of a contract of carriage providing for deck stowage. The exceptions come under the purview of the 1893 Harter Act,[3] which also governs all waterborne transportation in U.S. domestic service—that is, service on inland U.S. waterways (the Mississippi and other river systems, the Great Lakes and the coast-hugging Intercoastal Wa-

---

1 Also applicable to traffic between the mainland U.S. and the state of Hawaii, as well as to traffic between the U.S. and such possessions as Puerto Rico, the Virgin Islands, etc.
2 46 U.S.C. §§ 1300-1315.
3 46 U.S.C. §§ 190-196.

terway) as well as ocean service from one U.S. port to another U.S. port.[4]

In addition, both U.S. and foreign water carriers are always subject to the Harter Act during that period when goods that have been transferred to their custody are waiting to be loaded aboard ship, or after the goods have been unloaded but before their custody has formally been transferred to another party.

In most respects the liability regimes of the Harter Act and COGSA are coextensive. COGSA, however, is more favorable to carriers in one respect—its incorporation of a fixed dollar limit to carrier liability for loss and damage (*see below*). For that reason, COGSA is generally made applicable to *all* waterborne transportation by means of contractual reference. That is, as a practical matter virtually all water carriage touching at points in the U.S., both domestic and international, is subject to COGSA.

Under the Harter Act, water carrier liability (in both domestic and international operations) commences at the moment goods are transferred (with proper shipping instructions) to the custody of either (1) the carrier itself, or, more usually, (2) carrier agents or third parties, such as stevedores, whose activities are performed in connection with and as an integral part of waterborne transportation. Liability does not come to an end until the transportation process is completed, which is deemed likewise to include stevedoring and in some instances over-the-road dray services.

COGSA does not extend by its own terms to stevedoring and/or dray operations. However, to accord themselves the benefit of the liability limits, carriers ordinarily include so-called Himalaya clauses[5] in their bill of lading contracts which extend COGSA liability to these activities as well. It is important to

---

4 With the exceptions noted above.
5 The bizarre-seeming names popularly given to various contractual clauses, legal doctrines, etc.—the alert reader will note other examples through the book—derive not from any effort to be descriptive of their purport, but rather from the names of court cases that gave rise to them.

note, though, that such a specific contractual proviso is necessary before any dollar limits apply to carrier liability on or beyond the pier, or to parties other than the carrier itself or its employees or legal agents; otherwise the Harter Act, which incorporates no such limits, applies.

Water carriers are obliged to "exercise due diligence [to] properly equip, man, provision, and outfit [the] vessel, and to make said vessel seaworthy and capable of performing her intended voyage,"[6] and to "make the holds, refrigerating and cooling chambers and all other parts of the ship in which goods are carried fit and safe for their reception, carriage and preservation."[7] In addition, the carrier must "properly and carefully load, handle, stow, carry, keep, care for and discharge the goods carried."[8] Because these are affirmative duties imposed on the carrier, it must, in any dispute, prove it has discharged them.

The requirement for proper stowage of the goods has been construed to require stowage below decks; unless the bill of lading specifically provides for it, stowage of cargo on deck is deemed a "deviation," generally (although courts have carved out a few exceptions) rendering the carrier liable in the event of loss or damage. However, this applies only to bulk and loose (*i.e.*, uncontainerized) cargo; container vessels are intended to carry intermodal containers in deck storage, which is deemed in law to be no less secure than below-decks storage and is therefore not a deviation.

COGSA lists 17 exceptions to its regime of carrier liability. In substantial part this follows, albeit often in more detailed form, the five basic exceptions which apply to overland U.S. transportation (*see above*); but in some instances water carriers are exonerated from liability where overland carriers would not be.

---

6   Harter Act, 46 U.S.C. § 191; COGSA speaks similarly.
7   COGSA, 46 U.S.C. § 1303; the Harter Act is less specific, but its language is broad enough to encompass these requirements.
8   *Ibid.*

The list of exceptions reads as follows (with additional commentary where appropriate):[9]

(1) "Act, neglect or default of the master, mariner, pilot, or the servants of the carrier in the navigation of in the management of the ship."

(This is far and away the broadest and most controversial of the exceptions. Quite literally, the captain can steer the ship onto a reef while blind drunk and the carrier will have no liability for the loss of the cargo. The thesis on which this rests is that the owners of the vessel cannot exercise control over the ship's captain and crew while it's at sea, which may have had validity in earlier times but is much less apt in these days of radio communication. Nevertheless, as with other aspects of transportation liability, the law has carried over by weight of legal inertia far beyond the circumstances it was originally designed to meet.

(A clear distinction must be drawn between the captain's and/or crew's negligence and that of the carrier itself. If loss or damage occurs due to the carrier's failure to meet its duty to provide a seaworthy vessel, or to properly man and provision it, the carrier cannot escape liability under this (or any other) exception.)

(2) "Fire, unless caused by the actual fault or privity of the carrier."

(3) "Perils, dangers, and accidents of the sea or other navigable waters."

(4) "Act of God."

(5) "Act of war."

(6) "Act of public enemies" (the term "public enemies" once again referring to foreign military forces, not common criminals).

(7) "Arrest or restraint of princes, rulers, or people or seizure under legal process." (The term "people" in this context refers to a duly constituted legal governmental body, not to mobs

---

[9] 46 U.S.C. § 1304(2).

or crowds; however, see also the exception identified as No. 11 below.)

(8) "Quarantine restrictions."

(9) "Act or omission of the shipper or owner of the goods, his agent or representative."

(10) "Strikes or lockouts or stoppages or restraint of labor from whatever cause, whether partial or general." (However, COGSA also expressly provides that this exception is not to be construed "to relieve a carrier from responsibility for the carrier's own acts." Quite clearly, for example, loss or damage to cargo resulting from a lockout by the carrier of its own employees in connection with a labor dispute would not fall under this exception.)

(11) "Riots or civil commotions." (The extent to which this and/or the other COGSA exceptions, such as those identified as Nos. 6, 7, 10 or 17, applies to acts of politically motivated terrorism or sabotage has not been fully defined by the courts. However, in the author's opinion it is unlikely that water carriers would be held liable in such circumstances.)

(12) "Saving or attempting to save life or property at sea." (See also, however, the discussion of "general average" below.)

(13) "Wastage in bulk or weight or any other loss or damage arising from inherent defect, quality or vice of the goods."

(14) "Insufficiency of packing."

(15) "Insufficiency or inadequacy of marks" (*i.e.*, marking or identification of shipping containers).

(16) "Latent defects not discoverable [by the carrier] by due diligence."

(17) "Any other cause arising without actual fault and privity of the carrier and without the fault or neglect of the agents or servants of the carrier." (However, if the carrier claims this exception it has "the burden of proof. . . to show that neither the actual fault or privity of the carrier nor the fault or neglect of the agents or servants of the carrier contributed to the loss or damages." And, as with overland domestic transportation, even

contributory negligence on the part of the carrier will suffice to fix liability wholly on it.)

Although these exceptions serve to exculpate the carrier from liability, there are nevertheless times when the owner of lost or damaged goods may secure partial recovery from other *shippers* whose goods were carried on the same voyage, under the concept of general average. This arises when the loss/damage resulted from an attempt to save lives or property at sea. Examples include jettisoning cargo or beaching the vessel to prevent it from sinking, water or chemical damage incurred in fighting a shipboard fire, rescue efforts in connection with another vessel that's in danger at sea, etc.

In such instances the economic loss is pro-rated across all cargo carried by the vessel, and those whose cargo was saved are obliged to contribute indemnity to the owner(s) of the sacrificed goods in such portion that all risking property on the voyage bears the loss equally. A fairly detailed set of standards for general average claims is provided by the so-called York-Antwerp Rules, which have no formal legal status but are commonly referenced in bill of lading contracts.

As discussed, COGSA limits the carrier's liability to $500 "per package. . . or. . . customary freight unit," except where a higher value is declared on the bill of lading at the time of shipment.[10] This has created a good deal of legal controversy about what is and what isn't to be considered a "package," a question to which the courts have not yet arrived at any uniform, reliable answer.

In particular, the advent of containerization—which of course much postdates the 1936 statute—raises the possibility that the entire van-size marine container may be considered a single "package" for COGSA liability purposes, which in fact it has been in some court decisions. The general thrust of legal

---

10 46 U.S.C. § 1304(5); there is no similar dollar limitation set forth by the Harter Act.

precedent seems to be that the container will not be considered a "package" if (a) the contents are described in detail on the shipping papers, and (b) their internal packaging is sturdy enough that they could be shipped uncontainerized; but some courts have ignored these tests, and others have based their findings on just one of them. All that can be said with complete certainty in this area is that there is no clear rule.

Both COGSA and the Harter Act fix liability on the owner of the vessel or, where applicable, the bareboat charterer; however, in bareboat charter liability is *either* on the owner *or* the charterer, but not both. The contracting carrier is liable in the case of time charters. In addition, the laws also assign liability to the vessel *in rem*—that is, the vessel itself may be held liable, just as if it were a person, irrespective of any charter contracts, ownership, etc.

Of particular consequence in an era when intermodal transportation is becoming of increasing importance, there is no provision under either COGSA or the Harter Act for joint and several liability with carriers of other modes. Where shipments move in "land-bridge," "mini-bridge" or "micro-bridge" operations or some other variant of intermodal service, each participating carrier is liable only for the goods while they are in its possession. If the claimant is unable to demonstrate where the loss or damage occurred (a not-uncommon situation where the loss or damage was of a concealed nature), it therefore will be unable to recover from any carrier.

COGSA establishes a *prima facie* (at first glance) presumption of delivery in good order if the receiver accepts the goods on a clear delivery receipt. However, it allows a three-day grace period for the receiver to notify the carrier of loss or damage that "is not apparent"—*i.e.*, concealed loss or damage. And it specifies that neither a clear delivery receipt nor failure to timely report concealed damage is any bar to the filing of a lawsuit for loss and/or damage.

Suit may be brought in Admiralty Court *in personam*

(against some corporate or individual person, such as the owner, charterer, etc., of the vessel), or may be commenced anywhere the named defendant(s) may be served with legal process or anywhere it has (they have) property that may be subject to maritime attachment. Suits *in rem* (against the vessel itself) may be commenced in Admiralty Court anywhere the vessel is found. Individual or corporate defendants may also be sued in any court having jurisdiction over them.

It's worth pointing out that COGSA and the Harter Act apply equally to maritime freight forwarders, called non-vessel-operating common carriers (NVOCC). As that cognomen suggests, they are treated for legal purposes as common carriers on an equal footing with commercial shiplines, and assume the same liability with respect to their participation in waterborne transportation. Of significance, however, many NVOCC's also act as brokers, forwarders, etc., with regard to other modes of transportation, and in that capacity partake of the liability regime applicable to those modes.

COGSA and the Harter Act have long been sources of considerable dissatisfaction for shippers. The navigational-negligence exception, the per-package liability limitation, the lack of joint and several liability on intermodal shipments and the relatively short time period for the filing of loss-and-damage-related lawsuits are among the most serious complaints.

As of the time this is written (mid-1988), there were no fewer than three separate proposals for modification of the standards. The oldest and most conservative of these is the so-called Visby Amendments, an international agreement which dates from the late 1960's; it would raise the per-package limit (to approximately $750-800, the precise amount is based on fluctuating currency values) and would codify the loosely observed case-law rule that a maritime container will not be deemed a "package" provided its contents are itemized on the bill of lading.

The 1978 Hamburg Rules would further increase the per-package limit (to somewhere around $1,000) and likewise exclude containers from the definition of a "package" conditioned in B/L itemization; would void the COGSA exceptions in favor of a modified version of the common-law standard applicable to domestic surface carriers; would extend carrier liability to the entire time the carrier (or its agents, representatives, etc.) has custody of the goods; and would establish, for the first time, a standard holding water carriers liable for delay as well as for loss and damage.

Both Visby and Hamburg have been put in final form and ratified by some seafaring nations. The U.S., however, has ratified neither; and even if it does no changes in the maritime liability regime may take place until COGSA itself—which, by a very unusual provision, takes precedence over international treaties—is appropriately amended.

The most far-reaching approach is taken by the Multimodal Transport Convention developed under the aegis of the United Nations Conference on Trade and Development (UNCTAD). In recognition of the growth of intermodal transportation, the MTC creates an entirely new category of carrier, the Multi-Transport Operator (MTO), and, through it, establishes a uniform regime of origin-to-destination liability. By its creation of the MTO, however, the Convention departs somewhat from current commercial practices and procedures, and accordingly has had at best a lukewarm reception from the carrier industry.

Given the relatively restrictive nature of the maritime liability regime delineated by COGSA and the Harter Act, most shippers elect to purchase separate all-risk insurance for waterborne cargoes. A number of insurance carriers offer such policies at relatively modest rates; and in some cases coverage is provided through riders to the shipper's general business insurance.

15
Air Transportation

THERE ARE TWO SEPARATE LIABILITY REGIMES APPLICABLE TO air transportation, depending on whether the service involved is domestic or international. Or to put it altogether accurately, there is one regime for international service and a disorganized potpourri of standards in the domestic arena.

Between 1937—which is to say, effectively at more or less the inception of the commercial airline industry in this country—and 1978, domestic air carriage in the U.S. was subject to regulation by the Civil Aeronautics Board. The CAB required that carriers incorporate loss-and-damage liability provisions into their rate tariffs, and thereby effectively insulated them from the rigors of the common law applicable to surface modes of transportation. During the final decade of this period the Board took a yet more active role, and sought to prescribe rules which the carriers were required to put in their tariffs.

By the Aviation Act of 1978, however, Congress deregulated all domestic air transportation. This left no effective legal controls on air carrier liability; the CAB's rules were phased out by the statute (and ultimately the same fate befell the Board itself), but the common-law transportation liability standards were likewise, as a relic of the 40-plus-year history of regulatory override, inapplicable to airlines. Carriers were, and are, *de facto* free to pretty well establish their own standards for domestic service, based on airbill contract provisions.

Not surprisingly, most carriers promptly retreated to the

level of liability applicable to the ordinary bailee—*i.e.*, "warehouseman's liability," based on a negligence standard. There is, however, one signal difference: Because of historic standards of the air transportation industry it is incumbent on the air carrier to prove itself free from negligence in order to escape liability, rather than the shipper having to provide affirmative evidence of carrier negligence.

All other aspects of liability for loss, damage or delay are strictly contractual in nature, and vary somewhat from one carrier to another. Shippers must accordingly be alert to the pertinent provisions of airbills and/or carrier rate tariffs and circulars.

Most airlines restrict the dollar amount of their liability in two respects. First, they maintain a very low dollar limit—50¢ per pound is usual, often subject to a $50-per-shipment ceiling—unless the shipper declares a greater value at the time of shipment, and pays an "excess valuation" charge which may be substantially higher than the cost of purchasing separate insurance.

Second, most carriers maintain an "average value" rule where shippers do purchase excess-valuation coverage. That is, if a portion of the shipment is lost or damaged, the claim payment will be based on a per-pound pro-ration of the declared value for the total shipment. This will rarely inure in the shipper's favor, since claim documentation will ordinarily be required to prove the actual value of the loss and the carrier is within its rights in declining to pay more; but if the lost/damaged portion is worth *more* than the average per-pound value of the whole shipment, the carrier's payment under this rule is nevertheless limited to that average.

The law remains somewhat unsettled in this area (deregulation being, as of early 1989 when this is written, a fairly recent event); but it appears that in most cases air carrier liability will be treated by the courts as largely contractual in nature, and therefore not subject to judicial scrutiny except within the terms of the contractual agreement.

AIR TRANSPORTATION

Loss-and-damage liability in international air transportation is generally governed by the Warsaw Convention, a multi-lateral international agreement to which most countries actively involved in air carriage are signatory.[1] This applies not only on service between points in different countries, but also on domestic service performed in conjunction with an international movement—a U.S.-to-U.S. leg of an international movement on a through airbill, for example, or the same type of movement within the borders of a foreign country.

Under the Warsaw Convention the legal theory is, as with domestic service, that the carrier will be liable only for the consequences of its own negligence—and again the carrier has the burden of proving its non-liability. But the similarity stops here, because under Warsaw the carrier's proof must revolve around either one of the same five exceptions available to surface U.S. carriers (act of God, act of a public enemy, act of a public authority, act or omission of the shipper, or inherent vice of the goods) or some form of pilot error, for which the carrier will likewise not be liable; otherwise the presumption of carrier negligence will not be deemed to have been successfully rebutted.

A peculiarity of Warsaw's standards, however, may affect claims on shipments that require protective service (refrigeration, etc.). Where such shipments move overland, the shipper need merely specify that requirement on its shipping order; the carrier's failure to provide the protection will be deemed negligence *per se* (in and of itself, without need for further proof). If the carrier is unable or unwilling to provide the required protection, it must so advise the shipper and decline to accept the shipment for transportation.

An international air carrier, however, is excused from complying with such requirements unless it has expressly undertaken

---

1 The Warsaw Convention does not apply where the origin or destination of a shipment is located in a country that is not signatory to the Convention. In such cases (which are fairly rare) liability is based on the specific provisions of the contract of carriage.

to do so, such as by offering the particular form of protection requested in its tariff or rate circular. Absent such an undertaking, the airline will *not* be considered negligent for its failure to provide the protective service. Clearly this places the onus on shippers to familiarize themselves with carrier tariffs and/or to obtain contractual commitments from carriers to comply with requirements needed to secure shipments against in-transit injury.

Warsaw purports to establish a fixed monetary ceiling on air carrier liability; but unfortunately it expresses that ceiling in a manner that has provoked a great deal of controversy. In an effort to avoid value fluctuations and distortions of different currencies, the drafters of Warsaw saw fit to express the liability ceiling in terms of the "gold franc," an artificial monetary unit whose value derives solely from its fixed gold content. Specifically, a gold franc must contain precisely 65½ milligrams of 90% pure gold. Under Warsaw, the carrier's liability is limited to 250 such gold francs per kilogram, which works out to 16,375 milligrams of 90% pure gold, or 14,737½ milligrams of pure gold, per kilo.

For so long as the U.S. maintained a fixed parity with the gold franc (which lasted several years after the government decided to let the price of gold itself "float" on the free market), 250 gold francs was equal to precisely $20.00, establishing carrier liability at $9.07 per pound. When that parity was ended, however, it became problematic to construe the 250-gold-franc limit. Should it be calculated on the basis of the current market price of gold (which would raise the carriers' liability tenfold or more)? Or should the old $20-per-kilo, $9.07-per-pound limit be retained?

As of this writing (early 1989), these questions had not been judicially resolved. Indeed, in several cases reported to the author carriers had privately agreed to settlements substantially higher than the $9.07-per-pound level rather than risk an adverse court ruling.

> **The gold franc**
> To determine the precise value of 250 gold francs based on the market value of gold, multiply the per-ounce price by .473; that's the market-value-based carrier liability per kilogram. To determine the liability per pound based on gold's market value, multiply the per-ounce price by .2145.

Meantime, another international agreement, the Guatemala Protocol, has been drafted to eliminate this problem. Guatemala would replace the Warsaw references to gold francs with references to "special drawing rights" of the International Monetary Fund, another artificial monetary unit but one not based on gold.[2] This agreement, however, has not been ratified by the U.S. (nor by most other nations involved in a major way in commercial aviation), and thus the gold franc measure of liability still prevails.

Warsaw also provides for carrier liability for loss or damage due to willful misconduct by the carrier and/or its agents or employees; but the burden is on the shipper to (a) prove the misconduct, and, inestimably more difficult, (b) prove it was willful. If it meets that burden of proof the carrier is liable for the full amount of the loss without limitation.

Under Warsaw the claimant's right to recover for loss, damage or delay is contingent on its filing of a written claim with the carrier. This follows ordinary practice respecting domestic overland carriage, but eliminates the claimant's technical right (seldom, if ever, exercised as a practical matter) to skip the claim process and go directly into court; the international air shipper has no legal standing to sue in court unless he has timely filed his claim beforehand.

Joint and several liability (*see above*) is assigned to air carriers under Warsaw; as with overland carriers, claim may be filed with either the origin or destination carrier and must be

---

[2] Guatemala substitutes 17 SDR's for the 250-gold-franc limit.

paid if the (unexcused) loss, damage or delay is shown to have occurred while the goods were in the custody of any carrier participating in the through movement.

In some instances the air carrier's liability may also extend to surface pickup-and-delivery dray service performed by truck lines acting as its agents. In general the airbill will be the determining factor here; if it covers the motor service (at either end of the air journey), it thereby extends the carrier's liability to that portion of the movement.

16
Intermodal Transportation

INTERMODAL SERVICE—TRANSPORTATION LINKING TWO OR MORE of the major modes (rail, truck, water and air) in through movement of individual shipments—has become of steadily increasing importance in both international and, to some extent, domestic commerce during the latter half of the 20th century.

The primary factor in the growth of this type of service has been technological progress in the design and engineering of cargo-carrying equipment, which allows movement via multiple modes of transportation without the necessity of transloading the freight itself. There are three major variations on this basic theme:

• Trailer-on-flat-car (TOFC), or "piggyback," service, in which over-the-road highway trailers[1] are loaded aboard railroad flatcars for long-haul movement. Pickup and delivery operations (and, very occasionally, some intermediate "bridge" service) is accomplished by hooking the trailers to "bobtail" power units and traveling over the highways.

Operationally, the advantage of TOFC service lies in the comparatively lower variable cost of long-distance rail service. This derives principally from the reduced requirements for motive power per unit of cargo capacity, a factor that became more important in the early 1970's when the cost of energy shot abruptly (and steeply) up.

---

1   Most are specially reinforced to withstand the added physical stresses of railroad movement.

There are eight different defined forms, or "plans," of piggyback service:

Plan I—essentially substituted rail-for-motor service; the railroad acts as sub-contractor for the motor carrier in providing the long-haul service. Very rarely employed.

Plan II—railroad-provided service, with the railroad arranging for highway dray service at both pickup and delivery ends of the long-haul rail movement.

Plan II¼—same as Plan II, except the railroad provides dray service only at the origin end of the move; delivery is made at the railroad's destination ramp.

Plan II½—same as Plan II, except the railroad provides no dray service at either end; the movement is ramp-to-ramp only.

Plan II¾—same as Plan II, except the railroad provides dray service only at the destination end of the move; the shipper must arrange to dray the trailer to the railroad's origin ramp.

Plan III—same as Plan II½, except in shipper-owned trailers.

Plan IV—same as Plan II½, except that the shipper furnishes both trailers and flatcars. Also rarely used.

Plan V—coordinated interline service between railroads and motor carriers under joint-rate arrangements; one motor carrier may provide both origin and delivery highway service, or it may be furnished by two different carriers. Rarely used as of this writing (early 1989), but possibly increasing as intermodal affiliation of carriers becomes more common.

• Marine container service, which employs structurally reinforced and waterproofed highway trailers with detachable wheeled undercarriages—"bogeys"—that may be loaded aboard water vessels (primarily oceangoing ships).

Two types of vessels are used—Roll On/Roll Off (RO/RO) ships where the trailers are on- and off-loaded on their own wheels, and true containerships where the loading and unloading

INTERMODAL TRANSPORTATION

is done by means of either shipboard or dockside gantry cranes. Containers are stowed both belowdecks and on the deck.

Overland, the containers may be reattached to their wheeled bogeys and hauled over the road by highway power units. Or they may be moved by railroad in either TOFC or its companion, COFC (container-on-flat-car) service, the difference largely relating to whether the bogeys are first reattached (TOFC) or not (COFC).

Containerized movements are sometimes also called "bridge" service. True "land-bridge" operations involve ocean carriage both before and after the overland portion of the movement. "Mini-bridge" and "micro-bridge" are names given to overland operations which begin or terminate the transportation, the distinction lying mainly in the overland distance involved.

• Road-railer operations, involving structurally reinforced highway trailers that can move over either roads or rail lines.

Road-railers were initially designed with both sets of bogeys —the rubber highway wheels and the steel rail wheels—permanently attached. This, however, proved economically crippling; the heavy rail undercarriages added too much to the trailers' tare weight to allow them to meet highway weight restrictions when fully loaded. Modern design incorporates detachable rail bogeys, alleviating this problem.

Because they must meet highway size-and-weight limitations, road-railers are necessarily both smaller and lower to the ground than are ordinary railroad cars. As a result they cannot be commingled with rail cars in train service, but must be run in "dedicated" all-road-railer trains.

In addition to these three major forms, some intermodal service also takes place in specially designed airline "igloos" (lightweight air cargo containers) intended also for truck or, occasionally, rail service aboard flatbed equipment. And some intermodal service also takes place on bulk or loose packaged cargoes which are transloaded from mode to mode.

Carrier loss-and-damage liability in connection with inter-

MANAGER'S GUIDE TO CLAIMS

modal service varies depending on (1) the type of contractual arrangement under which it is performed, and/or (2) the modes involved.

When the contract of carriage for the entire intermodal movement is with one of the participating carriers, which either itself performs or subcontracts all service, that carrier will assume origin-to-destination liability. Thus, in Plan I TOFC service the motor carrier assumes liability for both the highway and rail portions of the move; in all others except Plan V the railroad does so; in intermodal air service the airline does the same as to both the air and highway portions.

However, it should be noted that this liability extends only to the limits of the contract of carriage—the bill of lading or airbill—which will not necessarily be coextensive with the entire physical movement of the goods. In Plans II¼, II½ and II¾ TOFC service, for example, some or all of the highway dray service must be performed by the shipper or separately contracted, subject to entirely separate liability arrangements. In such cases it will be incumbent on the shipper-claimant to document whether the loss, damage or delay occurred while the goods were being moved under the intermodal contract; and its failure to do so will be fatal to its cause.

Maritime intermodal service invariably involves such separate contractual considerations, in large part because of the dramatic differences between the liability regimes applicable to water and other forms of transportation. Thus, each carrier will generally be liable only for loss, damage or delay that occurred while the goods were in its custody, even though the ocean carrier may have arranged for the prior and/or subsequent overland movements.

In Plan V TOFC service (the only form of true joint intermodal service subject to the Interstate Commerce Act), the carriers assume the same joint and several liability as they would if only a single mode of transporation were involved (*see above*). Joint service involving carriers of other modes does not incorporate such joint and several liability; again, the shipper must identify the carrier that had custody when the goods were lost/damaged/delayed and file claim directly with it.

Some intermodal service is provided under the aegis of third parties—shippers' agents, freight forwarders, etc. The same considerations governing third party liability in other cases (*see below*) apply to these arrangements, subject, however, to the claimant's retained right to file claims directly with underlying carriers.

17
Third Parties

THIRD-PARTY PROVIDERS—THOSE WHO PARTICIPATE IN THE TRANSportation process essentially as middlemen rather than as carriers—are taking on an increasing importance in the transportation industry in the wake of the economic deregulation of the transport modes that took place in this country in the late 1970's and 1980's.

The law distinguishes among third parties in varying ways, depending on the underlying mode(s) of transportation involved; but insofar as loss-and-damage liability for the cargo is concerned, there are only two basic classes—(1) freight forwarders, who assume in-transit liability for the goods, and (2) all others, who do not. However, it is important to recognize that (with one key exception—*see below*) what is important is not the *name* under which the third party provides its services, but rather the nature of the services themselves.

The freight forwarder is perhaps best described by the appellation accorded him in the maritime sector—Non-Vessel-Operating Common Carrier (NVOCC). Forwarders take on, *vis-à-vis* their clientele, all the duties and responsibilities of the common carrier save one: they do not provide the physical transportation services themselves.[1] Rather, they engage, on their own behalf (and generally independent of any control by their ship-

---

[1] Some forwarders do provide highway pickup-and-delivery service within a limited radius of their termini.

per-customers), the underlying services of carriers who furnish the instrumentalities of transportation.

By dint of their carrier-like role, forwarders via all modes were, prior to the advent of the deregulatory movement, subject to basically the same economic regulation as carriers. That is to say, those who provided the services of forwarders were legally obliged to represent themselves as such, and secure requisite authority from the appropriate regulatory body to do so; and those who did not so represent themselves and possess the regulatory authorization were prohibited from acting in that capacity.

Although domestic surface forwarders (*i.e.*, those employing the services of motor or rail carriers) have been largely deregulated, a residue of this regulated status remains in that those who continue to represent themselves as forwarders are obliged to comply with the standards of the Interstate Commerce Act respecting liability.

Air forwarders, like airlines, have been completely deregulated as to domestic service, although they remain subject to the provisions of the Warsaw Convention for international movements (*see above*). The maritime NVOCC continues to be subject to some, albeit considerably reduced, economic regulation by the Federal Maritime Commission, which imposes the liability standards of COGSA and the Hague Rules just as with carriers (*see above*).

Leaving aside NVOCC's, deregulation has now opened the door for those who style themselves by other names—brokers, shippers' agents, consolidators, etc.—to become *de facto* freight forwarders irrespective of the nomenclature they use to describe their activities. That is, such parties voluntarily accept contractual obligations to their clients that make them responsible for the physical security and/or the timely delivery of the goods, just as do forwarders, notwithstanding that they do business under other designations. Motor carrier brokers, in particular, have increasingly found themselves compelled by competitive pressure to assume L&D liability by express contractual undertaking.

It must be emphasized that the intermediary role of such forwarder-like third parties (by whatever name) does not in any way compromise the rights of beneficial shippers *vis-à-vis* the underlying carriers who provide the physical transportation service. In the event of loss, damage or delay, the customer of such a *de facto* forwarder may of course file claim with and/or institute litigation against the forwarder entity; but he also retains the right to take the same action against the carrier (or, in the case of interline shipments, carriers) that actually had physical custody of the goods while they were in transit.

The second type of third party is the broker, shippers' agent, consolidator, etc. (any name except "freight forwarder" may be employed) who does *not* accept responsibility for the goods' fate while they are in transit. Such a third party acts purely in an intermediary capacity, arranging for transportation services but not assuming any participatory role in the performance of those services. He may act on behalf of either the shipper or the carrier (in some cases the role will vary from one shipment to the next), and may provide a variety of administrative services—including in some instances the actual filing of loss/damage/delay claims—but is not directly liable for what happens to the cargo while it's in transit. The lack of a clearly drawn line of demarcation between these two categories of third parties can create confusion and problems—a situation that's aggravated when a non-forwarder third party assumes responsibility for the payment of freight charges even as he eschews L&D liability. In such instances many shippers react to loss, damage or delay by withholding payment of charges *to the third party*, in the mistaken belief that they are thereby properly employing "self-help" tactics concerning their unpaid claims (*see below*).

In fact, however, the shipper's obligation to pay the third party (who is *not* liable for L&D problems) is, in law, entirely separate from and independent of its right to redress from the carrier. The shipper may not exact a penalty from the third party for the carrier's failure to pay a claim any more than it could hold one supplier economically responsible for the defaults of another.

18
Contract Carriage

AS WITH MOST AREAS OF THE LAW, THAT DEALING WITH FREIGHT loss and damage applies only to "common" purveyance. In our society, government takes the position that it has an important role in establishing the standards under which buyers and sellers do business on an *ad hoc* or casual basis, for the protection of both; but it also leaves the parties largely free to contract with one another on more or less any terms to which they mutually agree.[1]

In transportation the distinction between common and contract carriage is somewhat confused, due to holdover regulatory constraints which, though they may seem anachronistic today, still exert legal force. Strictly speaking, the bill of lading (or airbill, or ocean bill of lading) constitutes a "contract of carriage"; but, paradoxically, such a document is legally required only for *common* carriage, and may be (and frequently is) dispensed with entirely in *contract* carriage.

Except for domestic air transportation (*see above*), the bill of lading/airbill/ocean bill does not, and may not legally, alter the basic level of liability assumed by the carrier; the applicable statutes and common-law standards discussed in previous chap-

---

1 There are a few legal restraints on this contractual freedom due to "public policy" considerations, including certain fairly minimal regulatory standards applied to some forms of contract carriage; but for the most part contractual freedom—with both its risks and its benefits—is unconstricted by the law.

ters govern. Only if carrier and shipper negotiate a separate "continuing" agreement—which generally covers multiple shipments over an extended time period, must be in writing, and (as to rail and ocean service) must be filed with appropriate regulatory authorities—is the carriage deemed to be truly contractual in nature and therefore subject to liability standards which may be at variance with those governing common carriage.

Where such contracts are in force, however, they arguably supervene common-carriage liability standards. It is unclear whether, in a contractual relationship whose governing agreement was silent on this question, the carrier would be deemed by the law to have the liability of a common carrier, or would be subject only to the much lower liability of the ordinary bailee (warehouseman); but that very uncertainty gives both shipper and carrier an incentive to spell out this aspect of their relationship as part of the written contract.

Contractual freedom in this area is all but absolute. At the lower end of the spectrum, it is a truism of the law that no party may "contract against negligence"—that is, contractually relieve itself from the consequences of its own negligence. But like many truisms, this is fraught with exceptions, to the extent that carriers may *de facto* immunize themselves against virtually any possibility of a successful loss/damage/delay claim through contractual agreements.

At the other extreme, carriers may even contractually bargain away the exceptions to their "virtual insuror" role to which the law would entitle them if they were doing business as common, rather than contract, carriers.

As a practical matter, most real-world transportation contracts fall somewhere between these two poles. Typically the carrier will accept the basic common-law liability standard, but with an expanded *force majeure* exclusion to also cover loss, damage or delay resulting from such things as riots and other civil disturbances, labor strikes, acts of political sabotage or terrorism, etc. There will frequently also be some dollar-related liability, and/or "deductibles" that preclude the filing of low-value claims ($200-500 is common as of this writing). And some contracts also incorporate variants on the comparative negligence standard, where part (but not all) of the injury results from the shipper's or consignee's negligence.

However, a growing (although still relatively inconsequential) trend in contract carriage is for the shipper to agree to a limitation of the carrier's liability to that of the ordinary bailee—that is, only for the consequences of its own *proven* negligence—in exchange for rate (or, occasionally, other) concessions by the carrier. It's a trend that derives directly from the economic reality of the transportation industry.

In fact, as well as in name, the law governing common carriage places the carrier in the position of *de facto* insuror of the goods it transports. For the small carrier this imposes an all-but-intolerable risk; it is not unusual for a truckload shipment to be valued at several hundred thousand dollars, even $1 million or more, and even a single claim of this magnitude would overtax the resources of such a carrier. Moreover, the small carrier will lack the economic leverage to obtain affordable cargo insurance with low-enough deductibles to protect itself against such a catastrophic loss.[2]

For reasons associated with their accounting practices, large carriers, too, often find themselves in a not dissimilar position. Many carriers treat separate parts of their operations—individual

---

[2] A distinction must be drawn between this type of cargo insurance and the very different sort of coverage required of motor carriers by the Interstate Commerce Commission's regulations (Code of Federal Regulations, 49 CFR Part 1043). The ICC-mandated insurance is payable directly to the shipper/claimant, but only if the carrier defaults on paying a perfected claim for loss, damage or delay; it is first-dollar coverage (no deductible), but extends only to $5,000 per vehicle or $10,000 per occurrence. Common carriers *must* maintain such coverage (or secure ICC permission to "self-insure"); but many *also* maintain supplemental coverage for their own protection, subject to deductibles, to ensure partial reimbursement for large claim outlays.

terminals or routes, geographic areas, etc.—as independent "profit centers," thereby administratively impairing their capacity to absorb the cost of catastrophic claims (just one such could destroy the profitability of the "center" that incurred it).

Thus, either in actuality or by dint of the artifice of their internal structuring, many, if not most, carriers feel themselves severely threatened by the risk of a major claim. For this reason, and also because they may lack expertise in the actuarial risk assessment and valuation, they not infrequently exaggerate the L&D risk element in fixing their rates.[3] Thus, they may be willing to offer rate reductions, as tradeoffs for freedom from full carrier liability, that are several times as great as the probability-based economic worth of that liability.

In these circumstances it may benefit the shipper economically to either "self-insure" his own freight—that is, accept the economic consequences of any loss, damage or delay not attributable to proven carrier negligence—or purchase his own insurance elsewhere; his gains, in the form of rate reductions, will exceed (perhaps considerably) the anticipated value of his unreimbursed losses and/or the cost of his privately procured insurance coverage.

Obviously, this is an economic decision that must be made case by case, based on such factors as past claims experience, the "over, short & damage" (OS&D) ratio of the carrier in question, the rate benefit available, etc. It may also be advisable to supplement an agreement relieving the carrier of non-negligence-based liability with a contractual performance standard governing freight loss and damage, to ensure that its handling of the freight doesn't grow careless. But it is an option that should not be overlooked by the shipper.

---

3   The author encountered one situation in which a carrier agreed to a particular rate subject to the shipper's accepting a $100,000 ceiling on claims (about 15-20% of the actual value of each load)—but when it was unable to secure then-required ICC permission for this limitation, demanded *double* that rate in exchange for assuming full common-carrier liability.

A great many industrial traffic managers take the view that it is their legal "right" to recover from the carrier for loss, damage or delay occurring while goods are in its possession. With respect to common carriage, so, of course, it is. But that right nevertheless costs the shipper money, in the form of set-asides that must be built into carrier rate structures; and if, instead of buying "virtual insurance" from the carrier, a shipper can get *actual* insurance coverage elsewhere (or self-insure) at a lower cost, contracting offers it a freedom to trade off that right which it may pay to exercise.

19
Released Rates

TO SOME DEGREE THE CONTRACTUAL RATE-FOR-LIABILITY TRADE-off discussed in the preceding chapter is also available in connection with common carriage through the mechanism of "released rates."

A released rate is one the carrier offers contingent on the shipper's agreeing to some limitation in the dollar amount of potential loss/damage/delay liability. If the goods are lost, damaged and/or delayed in transit, the shipper is prevented from reneging on his agreement and claiming more than the agreed amount under the legal doctrine of *estoppel*.

"[I]f a common carrier gives to a shipper the choice of two rates, the lower of them conditioned upon his agreeing to a stipulated valuation of his property, if the shipper makes such a choice understandingly and freely, and names his valuation, he cannot thereafter recover [through a loss-and-damage claim] more than the value which he thus places upon his property."[1]

As this suggests, a released rate agreement/declaration has no effect whatever on the question of carrier liability. The carrier is, or is not, liable for any loss, damage or delay occurring while the goods are in its custody on the same basis applicable to any other shipment. The only effect of the agreement is on the *dollar amount* of the carrier's liability; it serves to fix a ceiling on the claim value.

In order for this agreement to be legally binding, three conditions must be met:

First, there must generally be some form of written agree-

---
1   *Union Pac. R. Co. v. Burke*, 255 U.S. 317.

ment, executed at the time of shipment, limiting the maximum claim amount. Most commonly this will take the form of a notation executed by the shipper on the bill of lading setting forth the agreed value (*although see below*).

No particular format of such a notation is required, *not even if the carrier's tariff purports to require specific wording*. It is enough if the notation is phrased with sufficient clarity to make the shipper's intent unambiguously clear,[2] and even generalized terminology will suffice. For example, some shippers have all their bill-of-lading forms pre-printed with wording such as, "All shipments are hereby released to the value at which the lowest freight charges apply," which serves the purpose quite satisfactorily.[3]

A common form of released value notation is to the following effect: "The agreed or declared value of the property is hereby specifically stated by the shipper to be not exceeding _____ [amount in dollars and cents] per _____ [unit of measure—weight, volume, etc.]."[4] There are two variants on this type of unit-based valuation which have a significant potential impact on claims.

If the valuation is stated just as above, the carrier's liability is limited only by the per-unit value multiplied by the total number of units (usually pounds, sometimes other measures of weight or volume) in the shipment. Thus, if *any portion* of the shipment is lost or damaged, the shipper may claim up to that ceiling amount. This is invariably the case with goods moving

---

2 *Strickland Transp. Co. v. U.S.*, 334 F.2d 172, and *Campbell "66" Exp. v. U.S.*, 302 F.2d 270. Cf. also *American Ry. Exp. Co. v. Lindenburg*, 260 U.S. 584.

3 Such language, and in fact any notation of this nature, regardless of the words in which it is couched, applies only to the extent that the shipper actually secures a reciprocal benefit in the form of a reduced transportation rate—*see below*.

4 Hoffmann, Stanley. *Model Legal Forms for Shippers* (Mamaroneck, NY: Transport Law Research, Inc., 1970, p. 116).

in bulk (not packaged or otherwise divided into discreet shipping units), and sometimes otherwise.

On packaged goods or shipments otherwise consisting of segregable items, however, the above language is often augmented by the addition of the words "per article" at the end of the phrasing—a specified sum of money "per pound *per article.*" In such a case each individual item in the shipment, in the form it is tendered to the carrier for transportation, is treated separately for purposes of figuring the maximum value of a claim. Thus, if one such item is lost or damaged, the carrier's liability ceiling is determined by multiplying the per-unit dollar amount of liability by only the number of units of measure of the lost/damaged item itself—*not* of the entire shipment.

This distinction may also be drawn by the language of the carrier's tariff, rate circular, contract, etc., even if it is not to be found in the actual B/L notation. That is, generalized language of the notation will be construed by the courts as an acceptance of the more specifically stated terms of the carrier's rate publication. It therefore obviously behooves shippers who use "blanket" value declarations to familiarize themselves with the particular terms and conditions of the rate publications of each carrier they employ, since they are stating their acceptance of such terms and conditions in legally binding language.

Alternatively, carriers may establish "default" released values in their own pre-printed bills of lading or receipts. This is the traditional approach of household goods van lines, parcel carriers and airlines/air forwarders, and is being increasingly adopted by other types of carriers as well. Provided that the shipper has an opportunity to declare a value higher than this standard (usually by paying an "excess valuation" charge), such provisions are legally enforceable under the doctrine of *estoppel.*[5]

But provisions of this nature, stated as a condition of trans-

---

5   *American Ry. Exp. Co. v. Lindenburg, op cit.*

portation *on the bill of lading or other document executed at the time of shipment*, are not to be confused with so-called "embargoes" on high-value freight published in carrier tariffs or rate circulars. In some instances carriers seek to force shippers to execute value declarations by specifying that shipments not released to a designated value (or less) "will not be accepted."

As a general rule, it is the carrier's right to so condition its acceptance of shipments for transportation. At the same time, though, it is the carrier's responsibility to enforce such tariff/circular provisions. If the carrier inadvertently accepts a shipment as to which no value declaration has been executed, it assumes loss/damage/delay liability up to the full actual value of the shipment notwithstanding any disclaimer in its tariff or circular by which it seeks to limit its liability; there is no basis on which to invoke *estoppel* against the shipper, and no other ground is legally available for the carrier to assume less than full liability.

In some instances carriers seek to avoid this problem by publishing "default" limitations in their tariffs or rate circulars, to the effect that shipments tendered without the value declaration will be "considered" as being released to the lowest valuation. A number of such provisions, for example, are incorporated in the National Motor Freight Classification pursuant released rate orders issued by the Interstate Commerce Commission in the pre-1980 era when such ICC approval was required by statute.

Carriers take the position that such tariff/rate circular provisions are fully binding on shippers, especially (although not exclusively) when they have been approved for publication by the ICC. However, court decisions issued to date (early 1989) indicate that these provisions are not *automatically* enforceable, no matter what the tariff/circular says. If a court finds, based on other evidence, that the shipper was (or should, by the exercise of reasonable diligence, have been) aware of the implications of not declaring a value on the bill of lading and made the choice anyway, it will consider the tariff-specified value limitation to be an implicit part of the B/L contract and the shipper will be *estopped* from claiming more.

Thus, shippers should make every effort to determine whether their freight is subject to this type of tariff or circular restriction. A shipper that has been prevented from making that determination by carrier actions—withholding copies of pertinent tariff/circular publications, misrepresentation by carrier sales personnel, etc.—will probably not, however, forfeit its right to claim full value.

The second condition that must exist before the shipper is *estopped* from claiming full value—in addition to the bill-of-lading declaration, in whatever form—is that the shipper must have received some tangible benefit in exchange for executing or accepting the value declaration. Ordinarily this benefit takes the form of a reduced transportation rate.

An obvious corollary to this is that carriers may not compel a shipper to accept less than full-dollar liability by publishing *only* released rates. This is expressly set forth in the Interstate Commerce Act,[7] and is even extended by the statute to service which has been otherwise administratively deregulated by the Interstate Commerce Commission;[8] and court rulings implicitly extend it to unregulated carriage as well (since a released rate can scarcely be deemed "reduced" unless there's a full-liability rate with which to compare it).

"The essential choice of rates [*i.e.*, one providing for full carrier liability, and a second, lower one based on a released valuation of the shipment] must be made to appear before a carrier can successfully claim the benefit of [a liability] limitation and relief from whole liability."[9] Unless the shipper has the opportunity to knowingly make such a choice, there is no *es-*

---

7 49 U.S.C. §§ 11707 and 10730.
8 49 U.S.C. § 10505(e), applicable only to railroad service; the Act does not authorize the ICC to administratively exempt service by any other mode.
9 *Cincinnati, N. O. & T. P. Ry. Co. v. Rankin*, 241 U.S. 319.

toppel against a full-value claim; any declaration of released value on the bill of lading is legally unenforceable against the shipper.

Further, the choice must be a realistically meaningful one— must have, that is, the result of actually reducing the amount of the freight charges. Thus, if (as is often the case) a carrier maintains the same minimum charge for released and non-released shipments, its liability for a minimum-charge shipment will not be subject to any *estoppel*-based limitation because there is no difference in freight charges.

An extension of this principle restricts the effect of a released value declaration when the declared value is less than the amount required to gain the benefit of the reduced rate. If the carrier's lowest rate is based on a declared value of, for example, $1.00 a pound, and the shipper nevertheless declares a value of 50¢/lb., the declaration is not binding to the extent that it might limit the shipper's claim recovery to less than the carrier-established $1.00-a-pound minimum.

In some key court decisions it has further been held that the differential in rate levels, released v. full liability, must be "reasonably related" to the economic value of the difference in risk assumed by the carrier. That is, the carrier may not inflate its full-liability rates so high as to economically embargo the traffic, and giving shippers no realistic alternative than to declare a released value—this is not the true "choice of rates" that must be offered. However, no cases of consequence have been decided by the courts on the ground that full-liability rates were too high to offer a meaningful choice; the author's opinion is that there would have to be a pretty dramatic disproportion between the rate and liability differentials before the courts would intervene on this basis.

Provided the requisite choice of rates is offered by the carrier, however, no particular *form* of such a choice is mandated. In particular, the availability of a greater level of carrier liability (up to full value) for payment of an excess valuation charge, as discussed above, is an acceptable manner of affording the choice of rates.[10]

Released rates must be distinguished carefully from actual value rates—those stated to apply on shipments having an "actual value" of less than a specified amount, subject to a declaration by the shipper to that effect (whereas released rates are based on an artificial "declared" value which is unrelated to what the goods are really worth). A false or erroneous value declaration by a shipper to comply with such provisions of carrier tariffs or rate circulars will not entitle him to the lower rate if the shipment is actually worth more than the amount specified; therefore a declaration in these circumstances does not *estop* the shipper from collecting full value in case of loss or damage.

However, in such a case the carrier may of course retrospectively collect freight charges applicable to the freight based on its actual value. Furthermore, if the value declaration was knowingly fraudulent (by a shipper seeking the benefit of the lower rate), it may legally bar the shipper from *any* recovery through a loss or damage claim.

Finally, even where the required choice of rates was offered and the shipper knowingly exercised it by making a declared value notation on the bill of lading, the carrier may not claim protection under the doctrine of *estoppel* if the loss, damage or delay resulted from its own tort (*i.e.*, civil wrong) or criminal act. That is, to take an obvious illustration, the carrier may not

---

[10] In his *Freight Claims in Plain English* (Huntington, NY: Shippers National Freight Claim Council, Inc., 1982 rev., p. 180), William J. Augello, executive director of the SNFCC, discusses briefly a case in which the New York Supreme Court held an excess valuation charge did not constitute such a choice of rates; *Dopico v. Transco International, Inc.* (unprinted; Jan. 15, 1975). The legal rationale for this decision is unclear, and may have to do with the particular dollar amounts involved being deemed unreasonable in proportion to the difference in carrier liability; in any event, this decision should not be read as a general disallowance of the excess valuation charge as a choice of rates, since contrary findings have been reached in many other cases up to and including the U.S. Supreme Court.

steal a shipper's goods and expect to pay the shipper only their declared (not actual) value. The same exclusion applies if the loss/damage/delay resulted from the carrier's gross negligence (a term that has been subject to numerous legalistic refinements, but fundamentally means in law just about what it means to the layman). It is, however, up to the claimant to prove such a tort, criminal act or gross negligence.

The use of released rates, in various forms, has increased dramatically since enactment of the various transport deregulatory laws beginning in 1978. Prior to that time the question of carrier liability for loss, damage and delay was subject to the control of the various regulatory bodies, and they were largely loathe to permit any limitations; only where a carrier's potential liability was so uncertain as to burden it with seriously unpredictable risks did the regulatory bodies allow publication of released rates.

The various deregulatory statutes, however, gave carriers freedom to establish such rates subject only to the controls of the marketplace itself; and they have exercised that freedom actively in the intervening years. Not only do they use this means of placing ceiling values on their liability (subject, of course, to shipper agreement), but there has also been growth in other types of limitations. In particular, it is not uncommon to find "floors" on claims, in the form of either deductibles (identical to those of insurance policies) or agreements that shippers will not file claims of less than a given amount. Further growth, and perhaps still more innovative approaches to the rate-for-liability tradeoff that is the basis for released rates, are probably to be expected as the industry continues to evolve in the market.

20
Responsibilities of the Parties

WHAT HAPPENS—OR RATHER, WHAT UNDER THE LAW AND IMPLEmenting regulations is *supposed* to happen—when goods are lost, damaged or delayed in transit?

As the law views this situation, it is to be dealt with through the joint efforts of all parties concerned. At the least this must involve both the consignee and the delivering carrier; and in many instances others—the consignor, the owner of the goods (if other than consignor or consignee), the origin carrier, any bridge carriers, third-party participants, etc.—are expected to participate as well. Certain duties and responsibilities are assigned the various parties, and they're expected to discharge those duties and responsibilities in a spirit of cooperation.

Logically, this is the only rational approach. All concerned have, in a real-world sense, been injured by the problem. Valuable goods are either gone altogether or, at best, have suffered a loss in value. The owner has thereby incurred direct and immediate economic injury; moreover, he, and perhaps others as well, face the problem of not having the goods available (at least on a timely basis) for their intended use. Meantime, the carrier(s) is (are) suffering the very real potential of lost future business because of the erosion of carefully nurtured shipper confidence; and there is, of course, the added possibility, even likelihood, of having to pay for the injury. It seems reasonable, then, that the parties should work together to resolve a problem that concerns them all.

Needless to say, this theory is rarely borne out in practice. Too often the situation devolves into mutual finger-pointing, with the two sides engaging in fruitless and debilitating recriminations as each casts about for ways of evading any further cost and/or inconvenience to himself, generally at the expense of the other.

To a great extent this sort of unpleasantness stems, not from misplaced ethics or an excess of cupidity in seeking to make others pay for one's own economic losses, but rather from an honest confusion about the division of duties and responsibilities contemplated by the law. Uncertain of what they *should* (each of them) be doing to resolve the problem, the various parties tend to make *ad hoc* decisions as they go along—resolving any doubts, not surprisingly, in their own favor.

At a practical level, however, much better results—for all concerned—can be achieved by adopting the more cooperative attitude envisaged by the law. This is especially true when the problem first manifests itself, and opportunities for correction, or at least amelioration, are available.

Shipments should be considered potentially lost, for example, if they do not arrive at their intended destination on or before the expected delivery date. Unfortunately, not all consignors or consignees keep close enough track of their goods in transit to be immediately aware of non-deliveries. But in any case, as soon as any party *does* become aware of such a situation it should be reported *promptly* to the carrier(s) by means of a "trace" form.

A trace should not be confused with a claim; in both a practical and a legal sense the two are entirely separate and distinct, and are intended to serve different purposes. The purpose of a trace is simply to apprise the carrier of the fact that part or all of a shipment expected to arrive at a particular place at a particular time has not done so—information of which the carrier may well be unaware—and to ask it (the carrier) to set in motion inquiries as to the missing goods' whereabouts.

Obviously, the more quickly these inquiries are started the

greater the likelihood of locating the missing freight, or, at least, of pinpointing where and how it was lost so that corrective steps can be taken for the future. But this depends on, first, the shipper's or consignee's willingness to keep track of its freight and make contact with the carrier about non-deliveries, and, second, the carrier's willingness to respond aggressively to such traces.

From the shipper's standpoint, a trace serves not only to alert the carrier to the need to locate missing freight, but also to protect its (the shipper's) legal rights if the goods cannot be found (or are found so belatedly as to result in economic injury due to delay). The time limits for filing claims and/or instituting lawsuits begin to run from the date on which (1) a shipment would ordinarily have been delivered, or (2) a partial delivery is made (*see below*); and it's obviously desirable for the prospective claimant to be aware of these dates as they arrive.

The author was told one bizarre tale of a rail carload of hops—the herbs used in the manufacture of beer, as well as other products—which disappeared in transit without anyone being aware of it. Not until more than two years later, long after the deadline for filing claims had expired, did anyone take note of the disappearance—when the now-desiccated load was discovered still in a car that had inadvertently been shunted onto a siding and forgotten. The owners of goods in transit should obviously take precautions not to so lightly lose track of them.[1]

The same holds true with regard to incomplete deliveries—where only a portion of the shipment arrives at destination. The

---

[1] Oddly, in this instance it would appear that the railroad, which was honest enough to notify the shipper when it finally located the load, had by its very integrity reinstated the claimant's rights. If goods are not delivered at all, the time limit for filing claims runs from the date of expected delivery (and had in this case long passed). But if goods are delivered in damaged condition, that time limit runs from the eventual date of delivery, no matter by how long delayed. Thus, once the railroad found the goods and notified the shipper, a new clock started to run on the claim.

carrier should be given as much information as is available about the missing portion, through a bill-of-lading or delivery receipt notation.

When goods are delivered in visibly damaged condition, it is, as has already been discussed, the responsibility of the consignee to accept delivery and seek to mitigate the damage as much as possible (provided, of course, that the goods are not so badly damaged as to be valueless). Once again, this potentially has an impact on the claimant's rights as well as having obvious practical consequences: If the consignee fails to abide by its obligation, the carrier cannot be legally held responsible for any economic damages that could have been averted had the consignee acted properly.[2]

As is the case with partial loss, any damage that's immediately obvious should be carefully and fully noted on the bill of lading or delivery receipt.

From time to time such notations cause a lot of fairly useless contention between carriers and consignees, due to misunderstandings about both their purpose and their legal effect. As with any document of this nature, delivery notations are merely archival records of the facts as those facts are known to the parties at the time the notations are made. They do not preclude either party from exercising any legal rights if it later develops that the facts are not as the parties then believed them to be.

Thus, the mere fact that a consignee has accepted delivery of a shipment "without exception"—that is, without any short or damage notations on the B/L or delivery receipt—does not preclude it from presenting a claim later on if loss or damage is subsequently discovered. Similarly, it is pointless for carriers to insist on a clear receipt because of disagreements with the consignee about the count or condition of the shipment; indeed, the legal process will be helped along if both parties document their

---

[2] Moreover, if goods are rejected by the consignee, the carrier will be liable for loss of or further injury to the goods only as a warehouseman until and unless it is provided with further shipping instructions.

RESPONSIBILITIES OF THE PARTIES

respective views at the time, so that factual disputes based on faulty human memories don't arise later to unnecessarily cloud the issues.

At the same time, it is inadvisable for either party to take the delivery receipt too lightly. Insofar as the facts are, or reasonably may be expected to be, known to the parties at the time of delivery, the receipt and any notations thereon will be exceptionally powerful and persuasive evidence should a dispute later arise. That is, a shipper who signs a clear receipt will face a steep uphill battle, at best, if it later seeks to show that the goods were visibly damaged when they were delivered; likewise a carrier who accepts a short or damage notation without making its own note of any disagreement it may have will be hard-pressed to argue afterwards that there was in fact no such shortage or damage.

This presupposes a fairly careful examination of the load at the time delivery is made. Many consignees tend to slight this step, especially on truck shipments delivered to busy docks where a managerial premium is placed on dock productivity. But with all due deference to the need for maximizing productivity of one's assets, it is an obvious mistake to give this so much priority that obvious loss or damage goes unremarked at the time of delivery; not only does that compromise the consignee's opportunity to later collect on claims, but it sacrifices the possibility of initiating prompt measures to locate lost items or mitigate problems of damaged freight.

Furthermore, a properly trained delivery-dock crew should be able to accommodate an adequate inspection of incoming loads without seriously impairing productivity. Indeed, for the most part this task is merely a matter of keeping one's eyes open and one's mind alert as delivery is accomplished.

Before unloading commences—whether it is the carrier's or the consignee's responsibility to unload—a representative of the consignee should make a cursory inspection of the carrier's vehicle, noting any significantly unusual features. Does the vehicle show signs of having been in a recent accident? Are the doors bulging, or is weather-stripping missing, so that the load may have been exposed to rain, etc.? Are braces, dunnage, chains, tarps, etc., properly in place? Is the load properly stowed? Is water, excessive dirt or other foreign objects in view in the cargo area? On temperature-protected loads, is the "reefer" (heating/cooling) unit working? And so forth.

This scrutiny should be accomplished with an eye to the bill of lading, shipment manifest, airbill or other documentation. In particular, attention should be given to whether the load moved under seal and, if it did, the condition of the seal and its serial number should be checked before it is broken and the vehicle doors opened.

It should go without saying that a review of the documentation should also include at least a brief glance at the identification of shipper and consignee, to ensure that the carrier is delivering the proper load; but some consignees neglect even this rudimentary precaution. The author was told of one rail shipment of bulk goods used in a manufacturing process that was accepted by a consignee without such a check. In fact the shipment was intended for another consignee located along the same branch line, and consisted of material that, although similar in appearance, was of a lower grade than that used by the consignee to whom it was actually delivered. That party, however, didn't discover the error until the delivered goods had contaminated the on-hand material with which it was mixed, and had even been used to produce one (defective) lot of goods.[3]

Where bulk loads are concerned, in some cases the consignee will require a quality-control sample before unloading commences. The results of such testing, by whatever means accomplished, should be retained as part of the delivery record.

---

3   Although the misdelivery subjected the carrier to some degree of liability, those additional damages resulting from the consignee's inadvertent acceptance of the load were not recoverable from the carrier (*see below for a discussion of such "special" damages*).

RESPONSIBILITIES OF THE PARTIES

Carriers delivering such loads should also insist on copies of those results being attached to the delivery receipt, for their own protection.

The same considerations apply if temperature or impact recorders, or other devices intended to provide evidence as to the treatment the goods received in transit, were employed by the shipper. The consignee should retrieve such devices and keep or record any information they provide; and the carrier should have the opportunity to examine the devices and/or get copies of records produced by them.

During the unloading process (or, if the carrier is responsible for unloading, immediately upon its completion) the consignee should take a *careful* count of any packaged freight. This is one of the most burdensome parts of the delivery process, but it is also one of the most important; if shortages are not discovered at the time of delivery it not only reduces the likelihood that the carrier can locate any missing items but seriously compromises the claimant's rights if goods are later discovered to be missing.

Where goods are palletized or otherwise unitized (on skids, slipsheets, etc.), however, it will generally not be necessary to break down the load fully for the delivery-time count—any more than it is necessary to open each carton or crate in order to count the contents thereof. The question to be answered at the time of delivery is whether the count of *shipping units*—be they boxes, pallets, items, etc.—corresponds with what the documentation shows was tendered the carrier at origin; the count need proceed only to the extent necessary to verify whatever information was available to the carrier when the goods were picked up.

Especially where the shipment has been transloaded or "platformed" by the carrier or otherwise commingled with other freight while in transit—almost always the case with motor carrier less-than-truckload shipments, sometimes in other instances as well—the counting process should include a shipping unit by shipping unit check of labels or markings. It is obviously not enough simply to verify that the carrier is delivering the same *number* of units it received from the shipper at origin; it is equally important that the units themselves are the same, and that the carrier hasn't inadvertently mixed up the freight.

The consignee should also check the condition of each shipping unit. Again, the opening of each carton, breakdown of each pallet, etc., isn't necessary at this stage (and will unduly delay the carrier if it's attempted, resulting in possible detention and/or other additional charges). But such an examination should involve *all* the senses—hearing, smell and touch, as well as eyesight. A carton that emits a telltale odor, or feels damp or oily to the hand, or gives forth a rattle or tinkle when it's moved, etc., may well have damaged goods inside. Any significant breaches in shrink or stretch wrap, broken rope or wrapping tape or metal banding or strapping, and so forth, should also be given attention.

In addition to noting any exceptions uncovered by this inspection on the bill of lading or delivery receipt,[4] the consignee may want to maintain photographic evidence. It is probably wisest to use a Polaroid-type camera for this purpose, so that the results can be checked immediately and photos re-taken if necessary; or videotape (with, again, the opportunity for immediate playback) will be quite satisfactory if such equipment is available. The objective, as with the documentary notations, is simply to establish the clearest evidence of the condition of the freight upon delivery.

Finally, if it all possible a complete examination of the freight should be made promptly after delivery—that is, the goods should be de-palletized, unpacked from cartons, etc., *even if they are not needed for use right away*. The effort, of course,

---

4   If space available on the actual document itself is inadequate for a full description, blank paper may be used and attached to the B/L or receipt. While it is obviously desirable to keep the description as brief as possible, enough detail should be included for a full explanation; it is better to err on the side of writing too much than writing too little.

is to uncover any concealed loss or damage quickly, while the best chance remains to reasonably show that the loss or damage occurred while the carrier had custody of the goods and not afterwards.

Some carriers maintain policies of declining all concealed loss/damage claims not filed within a specified time after delivery, such as the motor carriers' "15-day rule."[5] As already discussed, such policies do not legally affect the carriers' liability for concealed loss or damage, *provided* proof can be adduced that the problem did arise while the carrier had the goods. However, such proof will not be easy to produce; in most cases, in fact, it will be impossible. It is obviously preferable to avoid the problem as much as possible by checking the freight quickly so that notification of the concealed loss/damage can be given the carrier promptly.[6]

To be sure, there are times when this will be pragmatically unworkable—when, for example, the goods are intended for later reshipment in their original shipping cartons, when protective packaging is also used for display purposes in a retail establishment, etc. The consignee in such cases has little choice but to take its chances about concealed loss or damage. If an option does exist, however, unpacking and inspecting a newly arrived shipment should be treated as a priority.

---

[5] National Motor Freight Classification, Item 300135. The tariff rule does, however, afford the consignee an opportunity to "offer reasonable evidence. . . that loss or damage was not incurred by the consignee after delivery of shipment by carrier."

[6] Prompt notification of concealed loss or damage does not, of course, ensure that the claim will be successful. The carrier may defend on the basis that the problem arose either before the goods were tendered to it at origin or after delivery was completed. But the latter defense, at least, will be more difficult for the carrier if the consignee acts quickly.

21

Inspection

THE CARRIER HAS A RIGHT TO INSPECT GOODS ALLEGEDLY DAMaged while in transit, including any protective packaging in which they were shipped.

That right is subject, however, to a rule of reason; in particular, it must be exercised in a timely manner by the carrier. The consignee can scarcely be obliged to hold damaged goods, packaging, etc., in storage indefinitely awaiting the carrier's convenience to perform an inspection.

The law provides only that carriers must exercise their right to inspect with "reasonable" promptness. By tariff provision[1] the motor carrier industry has established a five-working-day standard for accomplishment of such inspections, which would certainly appear to fall within the boundaries of reasonableness in the general run of circumstances and will probably suffice as a rule of thumb for other modes as well.

The "reasonable time" allowed for the carrier's inspection does not begin until the carrier is notified of the damage. A notation on the bill of lading or delivery receipt suffices for this purpose; alternatively, and necessarily if the damage is not discovered until after delivery is complete and the carrier's personnel have departed the premises, the consignee may make a

---

1 National Motor Freight Classification, Item 300140.

separate notification. A telephone notification will do, but the difficulty of proving a phone call after the fact makes it advisable that a supplementary notice be given in writing.[2]

There will, of course, be times when damaged goods and/or their packaging cannot practicably be retained for five days, or even, in extreme cases, for as much as 24 hours. Perishable freight that has spoiled, for example, will produce noxious odors and attract vermin if not disposed of promptly. Other types of cargoes may be potentially hazardous in their damaged condition. There may be factors that mandate immediate repair of goods, either to prevent further deterioration in their condition or to avert ancillary economic consequences due to unavailability of the goods. And so forth.

In such circumstances it is incumbent on the consignee to advise the carrier of its reasons for not holding the freight for inspection. The consignee should then itself inspect the freight, and provide the carrier with a report of its findings; again, photographs and the like, as well as documentary descriptions, will be useful in this regard.

Similarly, if the carrier chooses not to exercise its right to inspect (or at any rate fails to do so within a reasonable time span), the consignee should prepare its own report. In these circumstances, however, the carrier is legally precluded from challenging the facts as reported by the consignee; having failed to exercise its right to inspect the goods itself, it must accept the consignee's report as its own.

If the carrier (or an independent representative engaged by the carrier for that purpose) does perform an inspection, it is obliged to provide the claimant with a copy of its report.

---

[2] Note that this notification of damage is all that is required of the consignee. The author once received a plaintive letter from a carrier claiming that it had been deprived of its opportunity to inspect damaged goods because, although it had been told the goods were damaged, it had not been invited to inspect them. No such "invitation" is necessary; it is up to the carrier, not the consignee, to take the initiative in arranging for an inspection.

22
Salvage

WHERE GOODS ARE DAMAGED BEYOND ECONOMIC REPARABILITY, it is up to the parties, once requisite inspections have been completed, to arrange between or among themselves for appropriate disposal of damaged goods.

If the goods are so badly damaged as to be practically valueless, this will generally pose no problem; they may simply be discarded. However, even this can create difficulties if the goods are subject to environmental or public safety restrictions as to their disposition. In such cases it should be recognized that both the owner of the goods and any other party taking responsibility for their disposal share liability, under the law, for any adverse consequences of their failure to comply with appropriate standards and requirements.

On the other hand, if the goods retain some economic value, the carrier has a right to demand that this value be realized to the extent that such act will serve to mitigate its (the carrier's) damages pursuant to a claim.[1] Most commonly this is accomplished by means of a "salvage" sale of the goods in their damaged condition or after partial repair.

In some instances laws and/or regulations, such as food and drug purity standards, do not permit such disposition. In such

---

[1] If realization of any remaining economic value will *not* serve to mitigate any damages payable by the carrier—if, that is, the carrier does not have liability, or if its liability is contractually limited to no more than the net loss even if the goods are salvaged—it has, of course, no rights at all in the matter.

cases, of course, the goods should be treated as economically valueless notwithstanding that they appear to be salvageable and that in fact a market may even exist for them, since they cannot be sold legally. However, some manufacturers and distributors are loath to dispose of salvageable goods for other reasons:

(1) They fear potential exposure under product liability laws if goods in damaged condition are sold to consumers who incur injury.

(2) They are concerned about possible injury to their commercial reputation if damaged goods bearing their brand or imprimatur reach the marketplace.

(3) They wish to limit availability of their products on the marketplace by restricting distribution to particular channels.

From the perspective of the goods' owner, these may be entirely valid reasons; it is not for the carrier, or anyone else, to judge them. However, whether valid or not, they are reasons that serve the owner's private purposes, and the carrier cannot be expected to subsidize them; if, on such a basis, the owner elects to scrap the goods rather than sell them as salvage, the carrier is nevertheless entitled to a "salvage allowance," equal to the net recovery that *would* have been realized had the goods been sold, as an offset against any claim that may be filed.

Some claimants argue vigorously against this, pointing out that, but for the damage that occurred while the goods were in the carrier's custody and care, there would have been no question of having to sell the goods as salvage at all. While this is quite true, the carrier is nevertheless responsible only for the *direct and proximate* consequences of the damage to the goods, not its indirect or consequential effects;[2] the owner must bear the cost of his own decision, taken for his own private reasons, not to recoup any remaining economic value of the damaged goods.

---

2   See below for a further discussion of "special and consequential" damages.

SALVAGE

Carriers will often agree to handle the salvage sale of damaged goods as an accommodation to their customers.[3] Although they will generally decline to do so if they intend *at that time* to disclaim liability for the damage, acceptance by a carrier of goods for salvage sale is not an admission or acknowledgment of liability, and is not admissible in law as evidence of such. Most large carriers maintain arrangements with commercial salvors for this purpose. However, it should be emphasized that the carrier is under no legal obligation to arrange for the salvage sale of goods, whether or not it is liable for the damage. It is the legal responsibility of the goods' owner to dispose of them in such fashion as will best mitigate the damages payable by the carrier; those carriers that undertake this function do so voluntarily.

Indeed, there are certain arguments that mitigate against turning goods over to carriers for salvage in certain circumstances. If the goods' retained value is high, it should be remembered that, during the time the carrier and/or its salvor has custody of the goods, its (their) liability will be only that of a warehouseman; should further damage occur then, the owner will have to prove negligence in order to recover for it. In addition, where specialized goods are involved it may be that the owner will be in a position to recover substantially more from the sale than will a carrier or salvor less familiar with the particular market in question; if such proves to be the case, the carrier will be within its rights in demanding a salvage allowance equal to the higher sum the owner could have realized.

If the carrier does assume the responsibility for salvaging the goods, under the law any net proceeds it realizes thereby are the property of the goods' owner *irrespective of the disposition of any claim*. It must hold that money in escrow until it can be passed on to the owner, along with a full accounting.

---

3   Item 300150 of the National Motor Freight Classification, for example, provides that carriers will undertake salvage sale of damaged goods "if [the] record conclusively reflects carrier liability."

As a practical matter, a convenient form of shorthand has arisen by which carriers who sell goods as salvage retain the proceeds for their own use, and simply pay the owner's claim in full. Ordinarily this will make no difference over the long haul, since in any event the amount of money paid out by the carrier and received by the claimant is the same (although in some instances it does lead to carriers' gaining several weeks' or months' use of the salvage proceeds while the claim is still pending).

However, this should be assiduously avoided in cases where the carrier is contractually liable for less than the full amount of the claimant's economic injury. The claimant is entitled to the full net amount of the salvage proceeds *before* any deductible or other limitation is applied to the claim amount. It is evident that if the carrier pays less than the full amount of the claim, its retention of the salvage proceeds will be to its distinct advantage.

23
The Value of a Claim

"THE BASIC THOUGHT UNDERLYING THE FEDERAL STATUTES [AND common law] which define the liability and prescribe the measure of damages in cases [involving freight loss, damage or delay] is that the owner shall be made whole by receiving the proper money equivalent for what he has actually lost, or, in other words, to restore him to the position he would have occupied, had the carrier performed its contract."[1]

That is, in seeking to place a dollar value on his claim, the claimant should consider first what he would have had, economically, if the goods had arrived without untoward incident—without loss, without damage, without delay. He should then examine what he now has, economically, due to goods having been delayed or lost in transit or delivered in damaged condition. The difference between these two sums, for all practical purposes, will be the proper value of his claim (subject, of course, to any contractual limitations on the carrier's liability).

In this calculation only hard, objectively provable economic injuries will be considered; speculative losses, recovery based on intangible or economically unmeasurable factors, etc., are not allowed. In particular, although in-transit loss/damage/delay will inevitably inconvenience (at least) the owner of the goods, and perhaps others as well, this may not be considered a part of the claimant's injury. Nor may carriers be obliged to pay punitive

---

1   A. C. L. Ry. Co. v. Roe, 118 So. 155.

damages under the law of freight loss and damage; this area of the law is intended merely to restore to the claimant the value of his economic loss, not to penalize the carrier(s) responsible for the loss, damage or delay.

In addition, the economic injury for which recompense is claimed must be the reasonably direct, proximate and necessary result of the loss, damage or delay complained of. So-called consequential or "special" damages are not ordinarily recoverable from the carrier unless it has specifically contracted for such liability (*see below*). Similarly, damages which could have been averted had the claimant (or another party having control of the shipment) acted as an ordinarily and reasonably prudent person, but were not, are not properly chargeable to the carrier.

Notwithstanding this seemingly straightforward and simple basis on which the value of a claim is figured, in the event such calculations often become the subject of bitter dispute. Claimants naturally seek to maximize, and carriers to minimize, the dollar amount involved; and there is often ample room for substantial disagreement based on peculiarities of the particular facts of a given case. Each sub-category of claim must be addressed separately in this context—although always with a keen eye to the basic purpose of the claim as being to make the shipper "whole," economically, for his loss.

24
The Value of a Claim—Loss

WHEN GOODS ARE LOST IN TRANSIT—OR DESTROYED (DAMAGED beyond repair or salvage), which amounts to the same thing—the relevant question to ask is, What were the goods worth in dollars and cents?

Unfortunately, few (if any) articles have a value that is fixed immutably in our market-based economy. There is often ample room for dispute on this issue due to different methods of figuring worth.

"The general rule," said one court in attempting a generalized answer, "is that, when goods delivered to a carrier for shipment are lost in transit, the carrier will be liable for the market value of the goods at the place of destination at the time when delivery of the goods should have been made. . . ."[1]

If this market value can be readily and accurately determined, it will in most instances be regarded as the legally applicable measure of damages. However, that determination must be based on known and provable facts, not merely speculation—the value that *would* have been realized through sale of the goods based on demonstrable conditions of the marketplace, rather than what their owner (the claimant) thinks or hopes with respect to their market value.

From this it should be obvious, first, that the market-value standard realistically applies only with respect to goods moving

---

1 *Anderson, Clayton & Co. v. Yazoo & M. V. R. Co.*, 141 So. 453, 455.

in connection with a planned or anticipated sale at destination. The value of goods moving for other purposes—raw materials intended for production uses, products moving for storage purposes, etc.—must be measured according to other standards more pertinent to those purposes.

The most simple such case would appear to be when goods were moving under the shipper's invoice, payable on delivery. In practice, however, this circumstance tends to evoke some of the greatest controversy in the entire area of freight claims.

Disputes generally revolve around the reality that commercial invoices will usually include an element of profit, which carriers are loath to pay—especially if, as is often the case, the customer to whom the goods were consigned subsequently accepts, in lieu of the lost shipment, a replacement order for which the shipper is paid its profit.

The law, however, is quite clear on this question: If a sale has been completed, to the point that the only remaining thing to be done to consummate it is physical delivery of the goods, the profit has *already* been earned by the shipper, and must be paid by the carrier as part of the claim if the goods are lost in transit. And this holds true without regard to whether a replacement shipment is made and accepted by the consignee, as to which the shipper may reap a *second* profit.

Where replacement shipment is made and accepted by the customer/consignee, carriers seek to invoke a standard on the order of "one sale transaction, one profit." They consider that the sale, *including* the replacement shipment, constitutes a single transaction, as to which the vendor/shipper has received its due profit (on the replacement), and accordingly feel it is improper for the shipper to include a *second* profit as part of its claim.

The proper legal standard, however, is better phrased as "one *shipment*, one profit"; and since two shipments were dispatched, only one of which generated a profit, the carrier is deemed liable for the unrecouped profit on the lost/destroyed shipment. With the lost/destroyed goods no longer available for sale, the vendor/shipper has incurred an "opportunity cost" equal to the profit potential on those goods, which he is entitled to recover as part of his claim.[2]

One of the leading court cases in this area involved a shipment of medication in a type of container known as a "carboy" (a large glass vessel encased in protective wickerware), which the carrier lost in transit. The court reasoned thus:

"It is true that plaintiff [*i.e.*, the shipper] delivered to the carrier [for transportation to its customer] a carboy of medicine to substitute for the one which was destroyed, but we do not think that the defendant's [carrier's] liability should be fixed at the amount required to reimburse plaintiff merely for the cost of manufacturing one carboy of medicine. What would be the situation if the second carboy had been lost, or even a third or fourth? Could plaintiff be required to continue to manufacture goods for the defendant at cost?"[3]

Another, and simpler, explanation of the rationale behind including profit as a proper claim element is based on the self-evident thesis that a carrier's liability should not be variable depending on such extraneous factors as the identity of the claimant. If goods are shipped f.o.b. origin, so that the consignee takes title when they are dispatched and is therefore their owner

---

[2] Note, however, that this does *not* apply if the goods are only delayed, or are damaged but repairable, and may be restored to stock by the vendor/shipper for subsequent (presumed) resale. In essence the vendor/shipper has merely exchanged one shipment (the original) for another (the replacement); its inventory is reduced only by the single shipment, notwithstanding that two were dispatched, and it is therefore entitled, by the one-shipment-one-profit measure, to only the profit it received for the replacement shipment.

[3] *Gore Products, Inc. v. T. & N. O. R. Co.*, 34 So.2d 418.

at the time of the loss or destruction, obviously the carrier will be liable for the vendor's/shipper's invoice price (including its profit element), which the consignee has to pay notwithstanding the in-transit calamity. How can it be proper for the carrier to be liable for less merely because terms of sale are such that the shipper owned the goods in transit and therefore it is he, not the consignee, who files the claim?[4]

As a general matter the profit on lost/destroyed goods will be considered "earned," and therefore recoverable from the carrier, only if the sale transaction had been completed except for physical delivery of the goods. In most instances courts will not award damages based on speculative profits—those that *might* have been earned through later sale of goods but were not contractually assured at the time of the loss or destruction.

There are, though, a few exceptions to this basic rule that have been carved out by courts over the years. One of the most important recent ones was the decision in *Polaroid Corp. v. Schuster's Exp., Inc.*,[5] in which the court awarded profit based on the "more than reasonable likelihood that the... goods would have been sold at the claimed market price" because of their popularity and the fact that they were at the time in short supply. A few other such cases have also devolved on the high proba-

---

[4] Indeed, if the rule of law were otherwise, it would merely encourage shippers and consignees to engage in "phantom" transactions regarding lost or destroyed shipments, in order to make the consignee the claimant and thereby permit greater recovery from the carrier.

[5] 484 F.2d 349. However, this case is well short of a true precedent for recovery of speculative profit even where the goods are selling like proverbial hotcakes. Polaroid's shipment (of film for its then-popular SX-70 line of cameras) was actually hijacked by thieves; and as the court pointed out, "hijacked goods, unlike those destroyed, ultimately compete with the manufacturer and, therefore, no true replacement is possible." It also observed that, since "Polaroid is the sole manufacturer of the types of products lost, all the purchasers of the hijacked goods would have had to purchase them from Polaroid." It was in considerable part to compensate Polaroid for the consequences of having to, in effect, compete with its own (hijacked) goods in the market, that the court held the company entitled to its not-yet-earned profit on this shipment.

bility of sale of the goods, even though no sale had actually been made at the time the goods were lost/destroyed.

A similar sort of exception applies with respect to goods that customarily move for immediate resale on an active "spot" market, such as, for example, fresh produce, grain, livestock, etc. The proper economic measure in such instances will be the going market price at destination as of the time when the goods would ordinarily have been delivered.

For the most part, however, where goods are not moving pursuant to a contract of sale, the value of the claim will be properly based on replacement cost. How much will it cost to procure or manufacture a new lot of identical goods? Where the shipment is moving, for example, to a distribution center, a warehouse, a retail outlet, a manufacturing facility for further processing, etc., this will be the proper claim amount.[6]

In addition, replacement cost may also be appropriate as a measure in unusual circumstances even where goods *were* moving under contract of sale. Many vendors maintain "loss leaders" as part of their marketing strategy—that is, they sell some articles at less than cost in order to gain ancillary benefits such as customer good will. Indeed, in some cases goods are actually given away to customers as marketing premiums. It would be ludicrous to suggest that the carrier should compensate a claimant based on the reduced loss leader invoice price, or even be liable for no damages at all in the case of giveaway premiums. After all, the shipper/claimant presumably expected to reap an intangible marketing benefit from selling below cost or giving merchandise away, of which the loss or destruction of the goods has deprived him; thus, the carrier should compensate him for the cost of replacing the lost/destroyed shipment.

---

6 The perceptive reader will have noticed that this is identical to the situation when claim is filed by the consignee on an f.o.b. origin shipment moving under contract of sale, as already discussed; the invoice value is equal to replacement cost.

Except in circumstances of this nature, however, invoice or market value will fix a ceiling on the claimant's recovery *even if replacement cost is higher*. This becomes of particular consequence with regard to one-of-a-kind items which cannot readily be replaced (if they can be replaced at all), or second-hand (used) articles of a type no longer being produced or widely available.

In addition, the underlying notion of replacement cost is based on like-for-like replacement. Thus, if an item has been used or has otherwise deteriorated due to the mere passage of time, replacement cost will be measured based on articles subject to the same prior usage and/or deterioration. If, as occasionally happens, there is no significant market in such items, replacement cost may be measured by the value of a new article of the same type, but with deduction of a depreciation allowance to accommodate the reality that the replacement article will be superior (in quality, expected useful life, etc.) to the one lost or destroyed.

25
The Value of a Claim—Household Goods, Etc.

NOT EVERYTHING BEING COMMERCIALLY TRANSPORTED IS AN "article of commerce," as the legal phrase goes. That is, there may be no real-world market against which to measure a lost or destroyed item's value.

In such cases—as with used household goods, *objets d'art*, etc.—assessing the proper amount of a claim for lost or destroyed goods poses special problems.

Sometimes the task will be simplified by virtue of a recent transaction involving the item in question. If the claimant purchased it but a short time before its loss or destruction, that acquisition cost will ordinarily be the sum required to "make him whole" economically for his loss.[1]

Notwithstanding that "secondhand household goods in use do not [usually] have a market value in the ordinary sense,"[2] there are exceptions. Definable markets do exist for used automobiles, major appliances (washers, refrigerators, etc.) and other consumer durables which provide a reliable basis for valuation.

---

1   Even this will not always be a valid approach if it can be shown that the purchase price is not an equitable measure of value. To take an extreme case, an art dealer or collector who picked up a painting for $10 at an auction and discovered it to be an original Rembrandt would scarcely be "made whole" for its loss or destruction merely by return of what he paid.
2   *Shikany v. Salt Creek Transp. Co.*, 45 P.2d 645.

For the most part this same basis will also be a sound guide for the value of used industrial and commercial articles, although items of exceptional age, character, quality, etc., may have to be considered on other bases.

Owners of furs, jewelry, silverware, works of art, antiques and the like will often have them appraised for insurance purposes, and such appraisals will be a helpful guide to their value. In some instances it will even be possible to have *ex post facto* appraisals made by expert review of photographs, descriptions, provenance, etc., of the lost or destroyed articles.

With regard to more ordinary household or personal items, it will generally be both impossible and inappropriate to base the value of a claim on any measure of the economic worth of the lost/destroyed article(s). Rather, "the fair value *to the owner* should be allowed," notwithstanding that it may exceed any amount the owner could have expected to realize by sale of the item. "If, for instance, a piece of household goods which has been used is substantially as good as new for all practical purposes, it would hardly be just that the owner should have compensation merely upon the basis of a secondhand piece of goods."[3]

Thus, in such circumstances the proper measure of value will frequently be replacement cost, notwithstanding that this is well above market value and may even exceed the original cost of the lost or destroyed item itself. Used articles of clothing, for instance, must be replaced by new clothes, used furniture by new, etc., in order to properly make the claimant economically whole for his loss.

This may even extend, if circumstances warrant, to *more* than what was actually lost or destroyed. It may be that the lost/destroyed item was a portion of a larger object which has been rendered therefore valueless (or at least less valuable). Or that item may have been part of a set, whose value is likewise

---

3   *Shikany, op cit.*; emphasis added.

diminished. In such instances the claimant may recover not only for the value of the lost or destroyed article but also for the reduction in value that loss or destruction occasioned in other, uninjured items.[4]

It has also been held that the carrier will be liable for loss in value of surviving articles only if it also transported those articles (in addition to the lost or destroyed article(s)); *Marcia Frocks, Inc. v. New York Dress Delivery, Inc.*, 29 N.Y.S.2d 322. However, it is far from clear that this should be considered a general rule.

In assessing value in such difficult cases, however, the rule is that only *economic* worth is to be considered; "mere fanciful or sentimental value" is irrelevant.[5] Thus, the fact that the lost or damaged item may have been a treasured heirloom, or otherwise greatly prized by its owner for emotional reasons, has no bearing on the proper amount of the claim. On the other hand, it may be difficult, especially in retrospect with the article in question no longer available for objective examination, to distinguish economic from emotional valuation (*See box overleaf*).

The same holds true, in general, for all types of extrinsic value—value, that is, which is not inherent in the basic nature of the lost or destroyed articles, but is rather of a particularized nature not subject to ready economic quantification. Lost documents, photographs, computer records, etc., may be of great worth to their owner, for example; but because that value is not intrinsic to the articles themselves, it will generally not be properly part of a claim. On the other hand, if the same materials

---

4 A puckish explanation of this was offered by the court considering a case in which one of a pair of antique vases, depicting the former King and Queen of Austria, was destroyed by a carrier in transit. Testimony was presented that as a pair the vases were worth $5,000, but the remaining vase (which happened to be the one with the Queen's picture) was worth only $1,500 alone. The court concluded that, "In porcelain, a widowed Queen is of less value than the wife of a living King." *Ry. Exp. Agency, Inc. v. Smith*, 212 F.2d 47, aff'g *Smith v. R.E.A.*, 110 F.Supp. 911.

5 *Shikany, op cit.*

> **The value of a rug**
>
> Miller's Law of Freight Loss and Damage Claims (4th ed., by R. R. Sigmon; Dubuque, IA: Wm. C. Brown Co. Publishers, 1974, p. 336) reports this entertaining exchange during testimony of a householder/claimant in a case involving a lost Oriental rug:
>
> "Q [by counsel for the carrier]: Tell the jury, in your opinion, what is the value of this rug?
>
> "A [by the claimant]: Well, value about $2,500 to me.
>
> "Q: I do not want to know what its value is to you. What, in your opinion, is the market value of the rug. What could you sell it for?
>
> "A: Well, in my opinion, it is worth over two thousand dollars to me.
>
> "Q: I do not want to know what it is worth to you. What can you sell it for?
>
> "A: I can't sell less than two—
>
> "Q (interrupting): It isn't what the rug is worth to you, it is, what can you sell it for?
>
> "A: Well, I will sell it for twenty-five hundred dollars.
>
> "Q: I want you to tell the jury what, in your opinion, was the value of the rug—not to you or anyone else, but what could you sell it for?
>
> "A: For twenty-five hundred dollars."
>
> *Shikany, op cit.* (In the event, the jury discounted this stubborn testimony and awarded only $725, a sum the carrier complained was still excessive.)

have an objectively measurable value—documents and photographs having historical significance or artistic merit, commercial computer software, etc.—the owner's damages are recoverable.

To sum up, there is no hard-and-fast rule about how the value of a claim is properly determined, especially where there are no readily available measures of the marketplace. Each case must be dealt with on its own merits, always with the objective of making the claimant whole for whatever actual economic loss he incurred.

26
The Value of a Claim—Damage

WHEN GOODS HAVE BEEN DAMAGED IN TRANSIT, THE VALUE OF the claim will generally be calculated by comparing two economic measures:

(1) The original value of the goods (*i.e.*, in the condition in which they were tendered to the carrier), less any residual or salvage value they retain in their present (damaged) condition.

(2) The cost of restoring the goods—through repair, refurbishing, repackaging or recoopering, etc.—to as close to their original condition as may be possible, less any loss in value resulting from shortfall in the restoration (impossibility or impracticability of restoring them to full original condition).

With respect to the latter, it's possible that there will be more than one alternative based on differing degrees of repair, quality of workmanship or materials, etc., each having its own economic consequences. In any event, the proper value of the claim is the *least* of the sums thus determined.

In other words, damaged goods may be repaired at the carrier's expense (*i.e.*, the cost may be recovered through a claim) only to the extent that the repairs serve to enhance their economic value in at least equal measure. If the cost of the repairs is greater than the reduction in value the goods have suffered in their present (damaged) condition, the owner will have to bear the difference himself if he chooses to have the repairs made anyway.

In extreme cases this may even mean that it is preferable to "total" damaged goods—declare them a total loss—than to have repairs made. This will not infrequently be so when the goods are of low value; it is less costly to mass-produce (or procure after mass production) a replacement load than to engage in the "hand-work" of repairing them.

What constitutes "damage," in the sense that it gives rise to a claim for economic injury against the carrier, will vary considerably from one case to another depending on the nature and intended use of the damaged article(s) or material. For example, it's obvious that waste material intended for recycling—scrap metal or paper, glass cullet and the like—can undergo virtually any in-transit abuse short of destruction without losing a jot of their value; whereas mere vibration can seriously harm sensitive electronic instruments.

Even injury to the packaging, without any hurt whatever to the contents, may qualify as "damage" for claims purposes if it causes economic loss to the goods' owner. Some goods move in packages designed to serve both protective and display purposes;[1] or, where bulk-type goods are concerned, intact packaging may be needed to maintain the integrity of the units, prevent contamination and infestation or otherwise maintain requisite purity assurance, etc. Or the packaging may itself be of intrinsic value, as reusable crating, pallets and the like.

As already discussed (*see above*), the consignee has an affirmative obligation to accept delivery of damaged-but-not-worthless goods and take such action as may be appropriate and necessary to mitigate the economic loss. His failure to discharge

---

[1] The author encountered perhaps the ultimate example of this in connection with a load of distilled water bottled in five-gallon transparent plastic containers for sale to consumers. Grit in the vehicle, coupled with in-transit vibrations that caused the jugs to rub against one another, caused extensive scratching of the containers, giving them (and their contents) a "dirty" appearance that rendered them unsaleable. The water was of course uninjured, but its value was negligible anyway; the load was a total loss because of the damage to the packaging.

this duty does not in itself relieve the carrier from liability for the actual damage; but if the consequence of that failure (whether a "necessary" consequence or not) is to in some fashion aggravate the damage, the carrier will be liable for the incremental injury only if it was legally negligent.

This is, clearly, of particular importance where the goods are of a perishable nature, so that time is of the essence in mitigation of the damage. Flash-freezing, for example, may serve to restore frozen goods that were partially defrosted in transit to good condition if carried out promptly; fresh produce that has partly deteriorated must be sold quickly to recover any residual value; and so forth. In such cases the law does allow the carrier to act unilaterally—*i.e.*, without approval or authorization of the owner—if the consignee rejects the load, but its actions (based on a lesser level of knowledge of both the product(s) and market conditions) may not serve to hold the loss to a minimum, and if that's so it won't be liable for the loss that could have been prevented by the consignee.

Having accepted the damaged goods, the consignee must give consideration to their salvage value *even if he has no intention of permitting sale of the goods as salvage* due to corporate policy or other such considerations. The net salvage proceeds that could *potentially* be realized, subtracted from the original value of the goods (that is, the amount that could have been claimed had the goods been lost or totally destroyed) will represent the maximum amount of recovery from the carrier; if the owner elects to make or procure repairs that cost more than this, he will have to bear the extra cost himself.

Repair costs must be "reasonable" to be recoverable through a claim. That does not necessarily mean the owner must exhaustively research alternative suppliers, but it may well mean he should get two or three independent estimates or bids and, if he chooses other than the low-cost one, be prepared to justify that choice from an objective standpoint. In practice, however, carriers will rarely question "outside" repair costs—those assessed by commercial suppliers of repair services—unless they appear to be exorbitant in relation to the work done.

The owner may also do the repair work himself, an option employed especially often by those who are also manufacturers of the damaged goods. Although carriers will often object, the law is that in such cases a "reasonable" overhead allowance, in addition to actual time and materials employed in the work, is permitted;[2] the owner can scarcely be expected to make facilities and indirect services available for the carrier's benefit (*i.e.*, having the effect of reducing the amount of the claim) without compensation. In some circumstances the claimant may even add a "profit" element to the cost of repairs he recovers from the carrier.[3]

In addition, any requisite inspections, testing, repackaging, recoopering, fumigation, etc.—just about anything that's needed to restore the goods to their original condition (or as close thereto as may be possible and economically feasible), provided always that it serves to mitigate, not aggravate, the economic injury—are likewise recoverable through the claim.

Repair may not, of course, serve to return the damaged goods to full original condition. In such a case the reduction in value is added to the cost of repairs, and is recoverable to the extent that the sum does not exceed the net loss in value suffered by the goods in the damaged condition in which they were delivered. Even cosmetic failures—inability to match colors exactly, etc.—are thus recoverable to the extent that they result in a proven loss in value. Again, however, only *economic* factors may be considered; sentiment and other emotional considerations play no role in placing a value on the claim.

Conversely, it may develop in some instances that the effect of repairs is to *enhance* the value of the damaged article beyond what it was originally. A piece of used machinery, for example,

---

[2] *Olcovich v. Grand Trunk Ry. of Canada*, 176 P. 459, and others.
[3] *Vacco Industries v. Navajo Freight Lines, Inc.*, 63 Cal.App.3d 262, cert. den. 431 U.S. 916.

if rebuilt, may have an expectable useful life beyond what it had in the condition in which it was shipped. Since the benefit of this enhancement inures to the owner, the carrier is entitled to an appropriate allowance in the claim.

This infuriates many claimants, who contend that they thereby wind up out of pocket for damage for which the carrier is legally liable. In terms of strict cash accounting, that's quite true. In the longer term, however, they may expect to recover their portion of the repair outlay through reductions in future repair/maintenance expenses they would otherwise have had to incur and/or through other economic advantages associated with the reality that they have, at the conclusion of the repair process, a superior article to what they had before it was damaged. The carrier's obligation, be it remembered, is only to make the claimant economically "whole," not to *improve* his circumstances.

However, once again any improvement in the condition of the repaired article must be a tangible economic one to warrant the allowance. For example, replacement of a used machine part with a new part would not be considered an upgrade if the original part would not ordinarily have been expected to wear out during the machine's useful life.

If the possibility of in-transit damage makes it necessary for the goods' owner to have them inspected—for possible damage, contamination, infestation, etc.—the cost of this inspection is properly includable in the claim.

However, the emphasis in the foregoing sentence is strongly on the word "necessary"; and the necessity must be integrally related to some untoward event that occurred while the goods were in the carrier's custody. That is, only if there is reasonable cause to suspect that the goods may have been damaged, contaminated, infested, etc., in the course of transportation is the consignee justified in claiming inspection costs from the carrier.

What constitutes such reasonable cause will necessarily vary according to the nature of the shipment and the indicator(s) that inspection may be necessary. For example, goods that require a high degree of purity—either because of legal requirements (as with foodstuffs and medications) or because of considerations related to their intended use—may have to be inspected based on only small evidence that they have been injured; a broken seal, a ruptured container, and the like may suffice. Hardier goods, on the other hand, may be treated more cavalierly and will not be properly subject to inspection without much stronger evidence of possible injury.

If inspection is performed under the circumstances described, the cost is properly includable in the claim *even if it develops that the goods are uninjured*. If they are shown to be injured, the inspection cost is includable in addition to the economic value of the actual injury.

27
Delay

CARRIERS ARE OBLIGED UNDER THE LAW TO TRANSPORT GOODS with "reasonable dispatch." When they fail to do so, and the claimant suffers economic injury in consequence, they are liable.

What constitutes "reasonable dispatch" is a matter that must be resolved case by case, based on the particular facts and circumstances that obtain. As a general rule, courts will use the "usual and customary" time required as a standard against which the carrier's performance on the shipment in question can be measured.[1] But also of importance are such things as published schedules, industry standards (to the extent they can be ascertained) and the like.

However, this standard may be overridden by express contractual agreement—*in either direction*. That is, the carrier may build into the contract (either specifically or by provision of a tariff or rate circular) a "cushion" allowing delay up to a certain span of time; railroads frequently do so in connection with the

---

1 *John Morrell & Co. v. Burlington Northern, Inc.*, 560 F.2d 277. "The carrier being bound to deliver in reasonable time, there could be no better standard for determining what was reasonable time than comparison of the ordinary time taken with that actually taken on that occasion." *Philadelphia & Norfolk R. R. v. Peninsula Produce Exch. of Md.*, 89 A. 433, aff'd 240 U.S. 34.

movement of fresh produce and other agricultural commodities.[2] Or it may voluntarily agree to a specified date and/or time of delivery, either implicitly (as by accepting a delivery appointment at the consignee's premises) or explicitly (by offering "guaranteed" delivery service based on a specified transit time—usually accompanied by some form of incentive or penalty provision.)

Delay is excusable if due to any of the five basic excepted causes that exonerate a carrier from liability for loss or damage (*see above*). There is, however, one salient difference: The "act of God" exception is considerably broader when delay is in issue, encompassing even foreseeable, ordinary changes in the weather if they're sufficient to force the delay. Thus, snow and ice storms, minor flooding, high winds and the like—which will not usually excuse the carrier in cases of loss or damage—will be deemed an acceptable excuse for delay if, for example, they serve to make roads impassable, render driving conditions unsafe or otherwise place insuperable obstacles athwart the path of prompt transportation.

A determination of what is to be considered delay is also inextricably intertwined with whether, and to what extent, late delivery of the shipment has caused the claimant harm. As one court put it, "Unexcused and unreasonable delay establishes a

---

2 Such a "cushion" was voided by the court in *Peter Condakes Co., Inc. v. So. Pac. Co.*, 512 F.2d 1141, as an unlawful limitation of the carriers' liability. After that case was tried (in 1975), however, the ICC administratively exempted most agricultural commodities from economic regulation under a provision of the Staggers Rail Act that also gives the carriers much greater latitude to contract on loss-and-damage claims matters (49 U.S.C. § 10505), and it's unclear whether and to what extent the *Condakes* precedent would govern present-day common carriage of such goods. Of course, it would not restrict them as to contract service save possibly to the extent the contractual provision purported to excuse them from the consequences of their own actual negligence.

> **Guaranteed delivery**
>
> Although guaranteed-delivery tariffs and rate circulars generally provide for full or partial remission of freight charges if the specified delivery schedule is not met, this does not preclude an injured shipper or consignee from *also* filing a claim for damages because of the delay. That is, the freight charge remission is not in the nature of "liquidated damages" such as might foreclose a shipper or consignee from claiming any *actual* damages he may have incurred; the two are entirely separate and independent.
>
> It should also be noted that in one long-ago case a court rejected use of a carrier's guaranteed delivery schedule as a standard against which to measure delay; *New York, Philadelphia & Norfolk R. Co. v. Peninsula Produce Exch.*, 240 U.S. 34 (1915). However, this was at a time when the only obligation on the carrier under the Interstate Commerce Act was to provide service with "reasonable dispatch," and such "guarantees" were not allowed in carrier tariff publications. Since current regulatory policy is to let carriers guarantee their service if they so choose, this case is almost surely not relevant in today's transportation environment.

wrong, but in the absence of proof of actual damage such wrong is not compensable under the Carmack Amendment [to the Interstate Commerce Act] or the common law."[3]

Thus, in at least one case a court found that a delivery only one day late constituted delay for claim purposes because of the economic injury suffered by the claimant (the shipment consisted of perishable foodstuffs);[4] whereas in others, delivery even weeks late has not been held to support a claim because there was no evidence of economic injury.

This last situation frequently causes consternation among would-be claimants. They consider that it is, or should be, self-evident that significant delay in transit hurts them economically, at the least by depriving them of the use of their goods for the

---

3   *Great Atlantic & Pacific Tea Co. v. A., T. & S. F. Ry. Co.*, 333 F.2d 705, cert. den. 379 U.S. 967.
4   *Lamb v. Ry. Exp. Agency*, 320 P.2d 644.

time of the delay. And in a real-world sense this point is hard to dispute.

But the law cannot deal with imponderables and intangibles; it must have specific, provable economic numbers before damages can be awarded.[5] And in many instances the only dollar injury a claimant can document will be of a collateral nature—equipment down-time, added labor costs, loss of prospective sales opportunities, etc.—that come under the heading of "special" or "consequential" damages and are hence not ordinarily recoverable from the carrier (*see below*).

The perceptive reader will observe that, if nothing else, the claimant has suffered by having its inventory tied up in transit for an excessive time, and should be able to recover that value. However, the claimant in such a case must be prepared to demonstrate that he would not have incurred that cost even if the shipment had not been delayed, and offsets based on storage and other costs must also be considered. Further, the amounts involved will generally be relatively small. Suffice it to say that the author is unaware of any case in which a court has awarded damages based on this sort of argument.

Where perishable goods are involved, delay may result in actual damage to or deterioration of the goods themselves. In such cases monetary damages are measured by comparing the expected condition of the goods at the time they would ordinarily have been delivered with their condition when delivery was actually made.

Even if the goods are non-perishable and are delivered, although late, intact and undamaged, the delay may still have caused a loss in value due to changes in market conditions. This is most evident in the case of seasonal goods—outerwear articles of clothing, goods designed for holiday consumption (Christmas cards, Valentine's Day and Hallowe'en candy, etc.) and the like. That is, the goods themselves may not have suffered deteriora-

---

5 "Remote and speculative" damages are not ordinarily allowed by the courts; *Critchfield v. Julia*, 147 F. 65, cert. den. 206 U.S. 593.

tion, but the market for them has; and the carrier will be liable to the extent their market value has declined.

However, the courts will generally not countenance carrying this beyond commercial reality. For example, the Christmas season brings greatly increased sales in a wide range of markets, but not all such goods are properly regarded as "seasonal." Such items as consumer durables may sell especially well during that period, but it does not follow that they become less valuable after Christmas has passed; a delay in transportation of such articles during this time of the year may thus result in little or no actual economic injury.

Some goods also have extremely volatile markets, with prices rising or falling literally from one hour to the next. Fresh farm produce falls in this category, for example. If, between the time of expected and the time of actual delivery, the fickle market has gone up, the owner receives a windfall; but if it has gone down in that interim, he may hold the carrier liable for any lost revenues.

In the event of delay, the carrier is duty-bound to notify the shipper to the extent that such notification is practicable.[6] If he fails to do so and the shipper suffers economic injury because of that failure, the carrier may be deemed to have committed a tort (*i.e.*, a wrongful act under civil law) and made to pay any resulting damages. It is pertinent that under tort law the carrier is *not* exempted from special or consequential damages if they can be shown to indeed have resulted from the tort. Thus, if the carrier's failure to notify the shipper of a delay resulted in damages *independent of the fact of the delay itself*, the shipper may sometimes recover damages that would not be allowed under the ordinary law of freight loss and damage claims.

---

6 This duty is spelled out in the Code of Federal Regulations (49 CFR §§ 1056.8(a)(2) and (3) with respect to ICC-regulated motor carriage of household goods, but is embodied in the common law as to all other carriers.

28
Conversion

CONVERSION IS "THE WRONGFUL EXERCISE OF DOMINION OVER another's property,"[1] and the carrier is liable on the same basis, subject to the same limitations and standards, as with regard to loss or damage.

Most commonly, claims for conversion arise out of misdelivery of the freight—delivery by the carrier to the wrong consignee, the wrong location, etc. The carrier has the same five primary defenses available as in the case of loss or damage (*see above*).

In making delivery the carrier is obliged to take all reasonable measures to ensure that the freight is being turned over to the proper party. Thus, carriers have been held liable when they have allowed thieves to pick up freight from their (the carriers') premises through inadvertence or carelessness.

Conversion claims also occasionally arise when the carrier is so misguided as to withhold delivery of freight in an effort to induce shippers or consignees to pay their bills or otherwise settle past obligations. In law, the carrier has a lien on goods in its custody only as to freight charges *on that shipment—not* on past shipments (or as to any other obligations, past or current). Thus, the carrier may refuse to deliver a shipment until freight charges on *it* are paid; but if it attempts to hold the shipment hostage in an effort to make other collections, it is guilty of conversion

---

[1] *Corpus Juris Secundum*, 13 C.J.S. Carriers § 181(a).

without regard to the validity of the bills it's trying to collect or how long past due they may be.

Occasionally carriers will find themselves in possession of freight that has been refused by the consignee. Terms of the standard-form bill of lading require the carrier to issue, to the shipper, an "on-hand" notice; and if the carrier intends to sell or otherwise dispose of the freight unless further shipping instructions are given, the notice must include an explicit statement to that effect. After waiting a minimum of 30 days after the notice was given, the carrier must still advertise its intention to dispose of the goods in "a newspaper of general circulation" at or near the place of intended sale "once a week for two successive weeks" before actually proceeding with the sale.[2] The carrier's failure to comply rigorously with these requirements may render it liable for conversion.

The carrier's failure to properly follow given shipping instructions may also give rise to claims for conversion. For example, if the shipper directs that the freight move on a C.O.D. basis ("Collect On Delivery," whereby the carrier is responsible for collecting payment of the shipper's invoice from the consignee), the carrier's failure to make the requisite collection at the time of delivery will render it liable. (*see above*).

As already discussed (*see above*), the owner of the goods also has the right of stoppage *in transitu*—that is, aborting delivery, a right that can be important if, *e.g.*, the shipper is the owner and chooses to stop delivery to a customer he has belatedly found to be insolvent—and a carrier's failure to comply with such instructions likewise renders it liable for any monetary damages on grounds of conversion. Orders for stoppage *in transitu* must be conveyed to the carrier in time for the carrier to act on them in the ordinary course of its operations. In addition, the carrier has both a right and a duty to demand proof of ownership from any party giving it such orders. Just as it constitutes con-

---

2   See section 4(b) of the standard-form bill of lading.

version for a carrier to refuse stoppage *in transitu* instructions from a party other than the consignee if that party owns the freight, so is it likewise conversion for a carrier to refuse delivery to a consignee if *he* is the owner. In the event of a dispute over ownership, the carrier is entitled to hold the freight until the dispute is fully resolved; and reasonable exercise of that right will *not* render it liable for conversion (or delay).

Theft is not legally conversion unless it is perpetrated by the carrier itself. This does not encompass theft by the carriers' employees unless it can be shown that they were acting in the course of their employment (*i.e.*, stealing was part of their job responsibilities). The distinction is largely moot in the context of freight loss and damage claims; although claims arising from thefts by carrier employees are considered under the category of loss rather than conversion, the carrier's liability, and the claimant's ability to recover for his economic injury, are the same. However, the carrier may not be held liable in a tort action for theft by its employees, whereas it does have such additional liability if it was itself responsible for the crime.

29
Discounts, Allowances and Interest

COMMERCIAL TRANSACTIONS IN OUR MARKET-BASED ECONOMY are not always based on a single-tier price structure. Vendors frequently offer discounts and allowances based on a variety of considerations.

Where invoice value is used as the basis for valuing a claim, this situation can arouse controversy. Carriers generally seek the benefit of all discounts and allowances, while claimants argue that none should be considered.

The truth, under the law, is somewhere in between. Because the sums involved are generally relatively small, there are few court cases directly in point; but consideration of the question in light of the standard of making the claimant economically whole for its loss will serve to develop some basic guidelines:

• Trade and volume discounts—those accorded a buyer because of his position in the industry or the volume of his purchases (whether on a per-order or period-of-time basis)—should clearly be deducted from the claim. Had the goods been delivered without incident, the buyer would have paid, and the seller received, a sum that incorporated these discounts; therefore, a carrier's payment of the claim without the benefit of the discount would go beyond what is needed to make the claimant whole. A limited exception must be noted, however, for claims involving only part of a shipment where the goods needed to replace the lost or damaged portion will not be eligible for a volume discount that *was* given on the original, larger quantity.

• Promotional and other allowances[1] granted by vendors for particular acts by customers are, on the other hand, *not* to be taken into account in valuing the claim. In essence, these represent a barter increment in an otherwise cash transaction, the vendor trading off part of the otherwise applicable purchase price in exchange for some other benefit. A promotional allowance, for example, is typically given by a manufacturer or wholesaler in exchange for the marketing benefit it secures by virtue of its customer advertising or otherwise promoting its goods; since the carrier will not be doing these things (and won't be incurring the costs involved in doing them), it is obviously not entitled to have such an allowance deducted from the claim amount. (It should also be noted that in most instances vendors demand "proof of performance," such as copies of published ads, before they will pay such allowances.)

• Cash discounts, also known by other names, are those extended to buyers as a consideration for advance payment of orders, or prompt payment of invoices after delivery. Since, again, performance is required in order to earn such discounts, they ordinarily will not inure to the carrier's benefit. Even if the discount was earned on the shipment in question, the earning of it involved some cost to the buyer—*i.e.*, sacrifice of the use of the money for an indeterminate period of time—which should be regarded as roughly equivalent to the value of the discount; since the carrier does not assume that cost as part of the claim,

---

1   The term "allowance" is used here to draw a distinction from other forms of discounting. In commercial practice this term and the word "discount" tend to be used more or less interchangeably; but the fact, for example, that a promotional allowance may be called a "promotional *discount*" by a particular company—or, conversely, that a trade discount is termed a "trade *allowance*"—does not change its basic character nor whether or not it should be credited to the carrier in a claim for loss, damage or delay.

it is likewise not entitled to the reward (the discount) that flows therefrom.

In this context the question of interest on claim amounts must be briefly addressed. As a rule carriers decline to pay interest, notwithstanding that the claimant incurs an opportunity cost equal to the earning power of the claim amount during the period that the claim is pending, which may be many weeks or even months. Where cases have gone to litigation, courts have in some instances awarded interest from the date of expected delivery or the date of the claim, but in others have dated interest only back to the date on which suit was brought. As a practical matter, claimants are generally going to have to accept non-payment of interest on claims that are settled privately, or else take their cases to court.

30
Taxes

CERTAIN TYPES OF GOODS ARE SUBJECT TO FEDERAL, STATE AND/or local excise taxes from the moment of their manufacture. And sales taxes apply in most jurisdictions to most types of business transactions.

The general rule is that taxes are properly includable in a claim for loss or damage if they constitute part of the claimant's actual economic injury. If, however, they are not payable by the claimant by dint of loss or damage to the goods—or, if already paid, are independently recoverable by him—they are not includable in the claim.

On tobacco products, for example, Federal taxes are payable the moment the goods leave their point of manufacture *under any circumstances*; even if they are stolen out of the plant, the taxes must be paid. Accordingly, these taxes will be properly part of a claim for loss of or damage to a shipment of such goods.[1]

As to shipments of alcoholic potables—liquor—the standards are the same, except that if the goods are destroyed or so badly damaged as to render them unfit for human consumption, the law entitles the owner to a remission or refund of Federal

---

1 Some states also assess taxes on this basis, although others have different standards. It may be that taxes will be payable in the state of origin on a lost or damaged load of tobacco, or they may even be payable in the state in which the loss or damage took place, or no state taxes may be payable at all, depending on the state(s) involved.

taxes.[2] In such cases the taxes are of course not properly a part of the claim.

Sales and other taxes are likewise includable in the claim to the extent tax liability was actually incurred by the owner on the lost or damaged goods. Other tax questions in conjunction with loss-and-damage claims must be viewed in this same light.

---

2   26 U.S.C. § 5064. Claim must be filed with the Bureau of Alcohol, Tobacco and Firearms (a sub-unit of the U.S. Treasury Department) within six months in such cases. However, even if the shipper fails to promptly file a claim and so forfeits his opportunity to recover tax payments, the taxes are still not recoverable from the carrier; the claimant's failure to exercise his right to recover the money from the government constitutes a default on his obligation to mitigate the damages, for which the carrier is not liable.

31
Freight Charges

"CARRIERS MUST, LIKE OTHER PERSONS, PERFORM THEIR CONtracts, and to recover compensation for such performance they must show performance."[1]

As this language makes clear, a carrier that fails to deliver goods tendered it for transportation in good condition is not entitled to collect freight charges therefor. If only a portion of the shipment is lost or damaged, freight charges are not payable on that portion; if the loss or damage involves the entire shipment, no freight charges at all are payable.

However, this basic standard is subject to one obvious exception; furthermore, it must be applied in the context of the totality of the claim itself.

The exception arises where a damaged shipment is repaired and then restored to the consignee. If repairs are carried out on the consignee's premises, it is evident that once they are made the consignee will have the time-and-place benefit the original transportation service was intended to secure for it; and since it has that benefit, it must expect to pay for it. To look at it another way, if the carrier waived or repaid freight charges the consignee would, at the conclusion of the repair process, have the goods on its premises at a *lower* net cost (*i.e.*, without having paid for transportation service) than it would have if the goods had been delivered undamaged. To be sure, the consignee may not have directly paid freight charges; it may not, in fact, even be the

---

[1] *Dunham v. Bower*, 77 N.Y. 76, 81.

claimant. But the point here is that if freight charges are waived or repaid in such circumstances *somebody* will have an economic benefit it would not have received had the goods not been damaged; and whether the benefiting party is the claimant or someone else, this clearly goes beyond the scope of reestablishing the economic *status quo ante*, which is the objective of the law in this area.

Even if repairs are carried out elsewhere, provided the goods are then returned to the original consignee the original freight charges are still payable, and unrecoverable, under the same reasoning. Of course, any costs incurred in transporting the goods to and from the repair site will in such circumstances be a proper part of the claim.

In addition, care must be taken to ensure that transportation costs are not *already* included in the claim amount, so that waiver or reimbursement of freight charges would constitute in effect a double recovery. Once again, the matter is generally most easily resolved if the parties simply examine the economic position the claimant would have occupied, had there been no loss or damage, and consider whether inclusion of freight charges in the claim amount is or is not necessary to bring about a restoration of that position.

A good rule of thumb is that the freight charges are properly included as part of the claim if (a) goods are lost or destroyed, or are to be sold as salvage or otherwise disposed of after having been damaged (rather than being repaired and then placed back in the hands of the original consignee), *and* (b) freight charges are payable directly to the carrier (or through a third-party intermediary) by the claimant. Otherwise, they must generally be regarded as being otherwise included—whether or not specifically stated—in the claim amount determined on the basis of other measures.

However, this should *only* be viewed as a rule of thumb, and exceptions must be recognized in unusual cases. In particular, where household goods are concerned (the purpose of whose transportation is not to enhance economic value), freight charges are recoverable without reference to this standard.[2] The same holds true with regard to released-rate shipments where the agreed liability limitation means that the carrier will not be paying the claim in full; freight charges are recoverable as a separate matter resulting from the carrier's non-performance of its contract, and are not covered by the liability limitation.

Occasionally shippers will replace lost, damaged or delayed shipments using expedited means of transportation, as to which higher costs are incurred than applicable to the original (lost/damaged/delayed) shipment. These costs may be included in the claim only if the effect of the replacement shipment was to otherwise mitigate the economic loss payable by the carrier—reduce the value of the claim—by at least an equivalent amount.

For example, suppose a damaged or delayed shipment is replaced by expedited transportation in order to preserve a sale that would otherwise be lost, the goods then being repaired (if necessary) and restored to the shipper's inventory for expected subsequent sale. The effect of the expedited replacement on the claim will have been to secure the shipper's profit on that sale, which is therefore not a part of the claim (*see above*); and the incremental cost thereof[3] is accordingly a proper part of the claim.

---

2 *Practices of Motor Carriers of Household Goods, etc.*, 126 MCC 127. But if the terms of the bill of lading were such that the shipper paid an identifiable incremental charge for an increased level of liability by the carrier, as with most household goods and many air shipments, this portion of the freight charges is viewed as the equivalent of an insurance premium and is not recoverable; *Petition for Dec. Order—Household Goods Freight Charges*, 114 MCC 176.

3 "Incremental cost" in this context refers to the difference between the charges for the expedited service and those for the original service, assuming freight charges for the movement on which the loss, damage or delay occurred are waived or reimbursed by the carrier. Had the original contract been fulfilled as contemplated, with no loss, no damage, no delay, the shipper would have presumably paid the freight charges on that shipment, so only the difference required to preserve the sale is recoverable as part of the claim.

MANAGER'S GUIDE TO CLAIMS

On the other hand, if the original shipment were lost or damaged to the point where it was no longer salable or usable as originally intended, the claim would include that profit element even if the consignee agreed to accept a replacement shipment (*see above*). Therefore the purpose of the replacement shipment would be to earn the shipper a *second* profit, the cost of which it should properly bear. This rationale would hold true even if the cost of the expedited service exceeded the shipper's profit (as might be the case if the shipper elected to replace the shipment, even at a loss, as a matter of customer relations); presumably the shipper would be gaining some non-economic benefit from incurring this loss, such as customer good will, for which it could not expect the carrier to pay.[4]

---

4 In *Freight Claims in Plain English*, 1982 ed. (Huntington, NY: Shippers National Freight Claim Council, 1982), William J. Augello offers one citation of a case in which replacement freight charges were awarded *in addition* to other damages—*West Bros., Inc. v. Resource Management Service, Inc.*, 1968 Fed.Car.Cas. ¶ 82,031. It is the author's opinion, however, that this should be regarded merely as an off-the-beaten-track ruling without precedential value; it appears to deviate too widely from the basic principle of making the claimant economically whole for its loss.

32
Administrative, Legal, Etc., Expenses

OCCASIONALLY CLAIMANTS WILL BECOME EXASPERATED ABOUT the costs they must incur in filing and pursuing claims, and will seek to recover those costs as part of their actual economic loss.

This attitude is certainly understandable. Various management efficiency specialists have estimated that the cost of preparing and mailing a single business letter, when everything is taken into consideration, can run as high as $20-25 or more; by this measure the cost of filing a more complex freight loss-and-damage claim and ancillary documentation is probably well over $100. In addition, the claimant may have to incur advisory or legal expenses in collecting on the claim.

However, such costs are legally unrecoverable. Even if the claimant is obliged to sue in order to collect on a claim, it will be unable in the ordinary course of events to recover the legal expenses it incurs thereby.

This obviously has the effect of discouraging claimants from pursuing claims for relatively small sums. Simply by obduracy, any carrier can make it impossible for a shipper to economically collect on such claims. However, the competitive realities of today's transportation market make it unlikely that carriers will abuse this situation, since shippers are fairly quick to stop routing future traffic via a carrier with a poor record of claims payment.

MANAGER'S GUIDE TO CLAIMS

By the same token, a carrier that successfully defends a loss-and-damage claim action in court will likewise ordinarily be unable to recover his legal costs from the claimant.

An exception to this standard applies to household goods shippers—appropriately, since such shippers are generally very infrequent users of van lines' services and hence lack the weapon of withholding future traffic to keep carriers in line. Under a program mandated by the 1980 Household Goods Transportation Act, shippers may in some circumstances recoup their legal costs if they must file suit to collect a claim.[1]

---

[1] See below for a more detailed discussion of this feature of the law.

33
Special and Other Damages

THE RULE OF "MAKING THE CLAIMANT WHOLE" FOR HIS ECONOMIC injury resulting from loss of, damage to or delay of freight extends only to what the law terms "general damages." So-called "special" or "consequential" damages, by contrast, are not recoverable by the claimant unless the carrier was given advance notice that any loss, damage or delay would or might result in such consequences.

Special and consequential damages are defined in law as "those which are the actual, but not the necessary, result of the injury complained of, and which in fact follow it as a natural and proximate consequence in a particular case, that is, by reason of special circumstances or conditions. Hence, general damages are such as might accrue to any person similarly injured, while special damages are such as did in fact accrue to the particular individual by reason of the particular circumstances of the case."[1]

Both the underlying nature of the distinction, and the reason that it is drawn, are implicit in the legal standard stating that "notice must be given [to the carrier] in order to recover special damages, or the evidence must show that the carrier had knowledge of the special circumstances, and this notice or knowledge must be at or before [the time that] the shipment is made."[2]

To expand, the general rule of law is that no-one will ordinarily be obliged to accept the proverbial pig in a poke as

---
1 *Black's Law Dictionary.*
2 *M. P. R. R. v. S. L. Robinson Co.*, 65 S.W.2d 902.

part of a commercial transaction. To the extent that any party incurs obligations and risks by making a contractual commitment, he is entitled, as the law sees it, to know the approximate scope of those obligations and risks beforehand. It would obviously be unreasonable to impose on any party "surprise" obligations of which he was unaware at the time he made his commitment, and which therefore played no part in either his decision to enter into the commitment or his formulation of the terms and conditions under which he agreed to do so.

It's the same basic kind of thinking that has led to so-called "lemon laws" giving buyers recourse against hidden defects in new automobiles, credit standards that shield consumers from undisclosed conditions of loans, etc. The law does not go to quite such extremes in protecting commercial enterprises (it presumes they're better able than private individuals to look after their own interests), but the same general principle applies: Anything that can't reasonably be said to have been within the contemplation and expectations of the parties when they reached agreement is not, as a rule, considered a part of their agreement.

Thus, a carrier is entitled to have a realistic idea of the economic consequences should he lose, damage or delay freight tendered him for transportation. He is presumed to know the value of the freight itself—not necessarily to the penny, but to a fairly close approximation,[3] so that in this regard he can realistically assess his risk. But ordinarily that presumption does not extend—cannot reasonably extend—to particularized consequences that may affect individual shippers. Accordingly, unless the carrier is notified, or can otherwise be proved to have known, ahead of time, he will not be liable for monetary injury resulting from such consequences.

---

3   If he does not, at least he has had the opportunity to obtain such knowledge through inquiry of the shipper, examination of the freight itself, etc. It's worth noting that one of the central factors used by carriers in establishing freight classifications and rates is the value of the goods.

In recent times there has been a dramatic growth in so-called "just-in-time" or *"kanban"* inventory management practices, whereby deliveries of inbound goods are timed to coincide with the need for those goods. Obviously companies benefit in several ways by not maintaining on-premises stockpiles; but the corollary is that the loss, damage or delay of even a single inbound shipment may have severe consequences—shutdown of a production line, loss of sale opportunities and the like, the costs of which may even exceed the value of the freight itself.

These things fall, however, within the classic definition of special and consequential damages; and the carrier will not be liable for them in the absence of the requisite advance notification or knowledge. The same holds true for the costs of crews and/or equipment held in readiness for unloading at the expected time of arrival of a shipment; costs associated with missing an ocean vessel's sailing date; the cost of finished product that has been spoiled due to in-transit damage to an ingredient; and other such losses that "in fact accrue[d] to the particular [claimant] by reason of the particular circumstances of the case" but would not necessarily have "accrue[d] to any person similarly injured."

As already mentioned, shippers may deprive carriers of their defense against claims for special or consequential damages by giving advance notice of the potential for such damages. Although a few courts have construed this requirement quite liberally, the prevailing view seems to be that the notification must be specific enough to give the carrier a reasonable opportunity to assess its obligations and risks with some degree of accuracy. That is, a mere notation of "Rush!" or the like will probably not suffice unless accompanied by some rough explanation of the reason for the rush and a description of the possible consequences if timely delivery of the goods, in good condition, is not made. In some cases it has even been held that the shipper should spell out the maximum amount of special/consequential damages, in dollars and cents. As a rule, the notice should take the form of an annotation to the bill of lading itself, making it inarguably part of the contract of carriage.

Realistically, though, any discussion of special-damages notations is to a considerable extent moot, since many carriers will not handle freight under these conditions. Some refuse such shipments outright, while others simply find themselves "too busy" to handle them; but either way the shipper will have great difficulty, at least, in securing transportation service. And in yet other cases shippers who give such notice are required to pay high excess-valuation charges that serve to discourage (at the least) them from adopting this course.

However, most carriers are unaware that they may also be held liable for special or consequential damages if, at the time they accepted the freight for transportation, they had—or might reasonably have been expected to have—knowledge of the circumstances giving rise to the damages. This holds true even if there was no notice given by the shipper; if the carrier knew what the situation was, the law will not cavil about how that knowledge was obtained.

A somewhat grisly illustration of this principle had to do with the express shipment of a severed dog's head, consigned to a medical laboratory. When still alive, the dog had bitten a young child; it was humanely killed, and the head was shipped to the lab so the brain tissue could be tested for the presence of rabies. The carrier delayed the shipment unduly, to the point that tests could not be carried out conclusively when it finally arrived; and the child had to endure the painful Pasteur treatment which was then the only known preventive for this almost universally fatal disease. The court held that the carrier should reasonably have known both the purpose of the shipment and the consequences of any delay, and awarded damages.[4]

Unfortunately, there has been some inconsistency by the courts in applying this principle. Some have been quite liberal

---

4 *Miles v. Am. Ry. Exp. Co.*, 233 S.W. 930.

in considering what knowledge the carrier had, or should reasonably have had, at the time of the shipment; others have taken a much more conservative attitude. Claimants have in general fared better where the shipment was of a specialized nature—used household goods, exhibit materials, agricultural commodities, etc.—than otherwise; but even this has proved no guarantee of success in court. This is an area where the quality of legal advocacy and the predisposition of the judge hearing the case may be of as much importance as the facts themselves, if not more.[5]

At one time, in the late 1970's, the Civil Aeronautics Board promulgated a rule making all air carriers and forwarders liable for special or consequential damages. However, by the time this rule became effective the 1978 Aviation Act deregulating domestic air service had already been enacted, and the CAB itself was ultimately phased out of existence a few years later. The rule no longer applies, and most airlines and air forwarders assume no greater liability for such damages than do carriers of other modes.

On a very few occasions carriers have also been held liable for punitive, or exemplary, damages. Such damages are in addition to what may be required to "make the plaintiff whole"; they are awarded where the defendant has engaged in practices deemed socially reprehensible, in order to discourage both it and others from engaging in such practices in the future. For the most part the cases in which punitive damages have been granted involved proven deception or fraud on the carrier's part.

---

[5] A number of such cases are discussed in William J. Augello's *Freight Claims in Plain English* (Huntington, NY: Shippers National Freight Claims Council, 1982 ed., pp. 153-167), which likewise demonstrate no clearly consistent underlying rationale.

34
Claims

BEFORE THE OWNER OF GOODS LOST, DAMAGED OR DELAYED IN transit may recover economic damages from the carrier, it must timely file a claim. Failure to do so within the time specified in the contract of carriage destroys the claimant's right to *any* recovery, even if the carrier is otherwise legally liable.[1]

A few exceptions to this rule are to be found in legal annals where extraordinary circumstances prevailed. In particular, if some act of the carrier prevented or dissuaded the claimant from presenting a formal claim, the carrier will not be allowed to profit (by being relieved of economic liability) from its misbehavior *(see box overleaf)*; and there are also a few court cases which hold that actual filing of a claim isn't necessary if the carrier is already possessed of all pertinent information. Such cases are quite unusual, however, and the decisions are not altogether consistent; the wisest rule is to regard the timely filing of a claim as absolutely mandatory.

To some degree the format of a claim may be the subject of a shipper-carrier agreement, such as by provision in the contract of carriage. The shipper may, for example, agree that only a specific form will constitute a claim, although such agreements are distinctly unusual. Or the carrier may agree to accept elec-

---

[1] This requirement may also be met in most (although not all—*see below*) instances by institution of a lawsuit within the contractual time period. However, it is obviously foolish to take on the costs and burdens of filing legal action where the mere filing of a claim may accomplish the purpose as effectively (and the right to sue is, of course, held in reserve).

> ### The case of the 'forced' B/L
> A curious case that came to the author's attention involved an LTL shipment consisting of several cartons moving in interline service. Some of the cartons were lost while the originating carrier had custody of the goods. That carrier was aware that its connecting line had a firm policy of refusing to accept, in interline service, shipments with exceptions notations. (Because such acceptance would render it potentially liable, under the concept of joint and several liability (*see above*), for any subsequently filed claims, this is not an unreasonable policy.)
>
> Accordingly, the origin carrier "forced" a new bill of lading which showed only the number of cartons which still remained. It did not, however, advise either the shipper or the consignee of its action, and it either destroyed or filed away the copies of the original (complete) bill of lading. The remainder of the shipment was duly delivered, seemingly intact (based on the new B/L), and as a result the shortage went unnoticed until the time for filing claims had long since expired.
>
> In such circumstances it was the author's view that the origin carrier's actions were at least partly responsible for the failure to file a timely claim, and that this failure therefore did not preclude the claimant's recovery.

tronically transmitted claims, which, in the modern era of computerization and electronic data interchange (EDI), is becoming increasingly commonplace.

Absent such an agreement, however, a claim need follow no particular format, provided only that it includes certain requisite information. A document is a legally valid claim if (and only if) it includes *all* of the following elements:

- Identification of shipper and consignee.
- Origin and destination of the shipment.
- Name(s) of the carrier(s) who handled the shipment, and/or routing instructions provided by the shipper.
- Date on which shipment was made.
- Date of delivery (if delivery was made).

- General description of the loss, damage or delay.[2]
- A statement to the effect that the claimant is seeking monetary damages from the carrier.

It is in the last-named area that most problems are encountered and most disputes arise about whether a particular document is or is not to be considered a legally valid claim. Especially, documents such as "tracers," delivery-receipt notations, damage-inspection requests and the like will generally not qualify as claims because they do not include this crucial demand for monetary damages.

Many carriers have proprietary claim forms, generally similar to that of Figure 1, which they try to insist that all claimants use. It will obviously facilitate the processing of the claim to use such a form; but unless there is a prior agreement to do so, such use is not legally mandatory. A claim may be as simple as the following form letter on the shipper's letterhead:

"You are hereby notified that on or about [date of shipment], we shipped from [origin] to [name of consignee] and [destination] a shipment of [description of shipment] covered by your [B/L number] which was delivered in damaged condition at destination on [delivery date]. For the damage incurred in transit, this is our claim for [amount]."[3]

Although the claim must demand payment of monetary damages, it need not identify a specific dollar amount. Sometimes that information won't be immediately available; it may take weeks or even months to determine repair costs, salvage value, etc. In such circumstances the claim may be filed for an uncertain amount, such as "$100 more or less," and completed—by spelling out the exact amount claimed—later on. The claim is legally valid even though the carrier may not be advised of

---

2   However, "the claim need not set out all the particulars of the damage [or loss, or delay]"; *Gay v. Graves Truck Line*, 573 P.2d 632.

3   Adapted from *Model Legal Forms for Shippers*, by Stanley Hoffman (Mamaroneck, NY: Transport Law Research, 1970), Form 78, pp. 254-5.

MANAGER'S GUIDE TO CLAIMS

the exact amount of damages until after expiration of the claim-filing time. (However, the carrier can't of course be expected to

STANDARD FORM FOR PRESENTATION OF LOSS OR DAMAGE CLAIMS

Approved by
THE INTERSTATE COMMERCE COMMISSION
THE NATIONAL INDUSTRIAL TRAFFIC LEAGUE
FREIGHT CLAIM ASSOCIATION

..................(Address of Claimant)..................

(Name of person to whom claim is presented) ....(Date)......... Claimant's Number §

(Name of carrier)..................

(Address).................. (Carrier's Number)

This claim for $........is made against the carrier named above by (Name of claimant)..................

..................for (Loss or damage)..................in connection with the following described shipment:

Description of shipment..................
Name and address of consignor/shipper..................
Shipped from (City, town or station).........., To (City, town or station)..........
Final destination (City, town or station)..........Routed via..........
Bill of Lading issued by..........Co.; Date of Bill of Lading..........
Paid Freight Bill/Pro Number..........Original Car number and Initial..........
Name and address of consignee to whom shipped..................
If shipment reconsigned enroute, state particulars:..................

§ Claimant should assign to each claim a number, inserting same in the space provided at the upper right hand corner of this form. Reference should be made thereto in all correspondence pertaining to this claim.

DETAILED STATEMENT SHOWING HOW AMOUNT CLAIMED IS DETERMINED
(Number and description of articles, nature and extent of loss or damage, invoice price of articles, amount of claim, etc.)

Total Amount Claimed

IN ADDITION TO THE INFORMATION GIVEN ABOVE, THE FOLLOWING DOCUMENTS
ARE SUBMITTED IN SUPPORT OF THIS CLAIM.*

( ) 1. Original bill of lading, if not previously surrendered to carrier.
( ) 2. Original paid freight ("Expense") bill.
( ) 3. Original invoice or certified copy.
      4. Other particulars obtainable in proof of loss or damage claimed.

Remarks:..................

The foregoing statement of facts is hereby certified to as correct.

(Signature of claimant)

* Claimant will please check x before such of the documents mentioned as have been attached, and explain under "Remarks" the absence of any of the documents called for in connection with this claim. When for any reason it is impossible for claimant to produce original bill of lading, if required, or paid freight bill, claimant should indemnify† carrier or carriers against duplicate claim supported by original documents.

Fig. 1—Typical claim form.

pay a claim until the amount claimed has been named by the claimant.)

In general, the claim will also have to be supplemented by additional information and documentation (although once again that need not be done within the time for filing the claim itself). Typically that will include:

- Evidence of the claimant's right to file the claim—its ownership of the lost/damaged/delayed goods, or proof that the owner has "assigned" all claim rights to it. As a rule the original paid freight bill or the original copy of the bill of lading will be deemed to constitute such proof.[4]

- Evidence backing up the value of the damages being claimed—invoices, repair bills, etc.

Some carriers will also harass claimants with demands for additional evidence or documentation. A simple rule is that the carrier has a right to any and all evidence legally required to establish its liability, the amount of that liability, and the proper party to whom it is liable—evidence, that is, that the claimant would have to produce in court if the matter became the subject of litigation—but may not properly use spurious requests for information that *wouldn't* be needed in court merely for the purpose of delaying payment of the claim.

It is crucial for the claimant to identify the proper carrier with whom to file the claim; a claim filed with the wrong carrier is invalid, imposing no legal obligation on either the carrier with

---

4   If documentation is unavailable, the claimant may execute an "indemnity bond" stating in effect that if, after the claim is paid, some other party demonstrates a better right to receive the payment, the original claimant will return the money. A typical indemnity bond reads something like this (the example is taken from *Model Legal Forms for Shippers, op cit.*, Form 80, p. 258):

   "In consideration of the payment of this claim in the absence of the original freight bill or bill of lading, we hereby hold the carrier and its connections free from liability against second payment due to our inability to produce the original freight bill or bill of lading, same having been lost, destroyed, or inadvertently misplaced."

whom it is filed or the carrier with whom it should have been filed.

Claim may always be filed with the carrier that had custody of the goods at the time the loss, damage or delay occurred (provided, of course, that can be proved). This holds true even where the goods were moving under contract with a third-party provider, such as a broker or freight forwarder that assumed in-transit liability for the shipment; the owner always has the right to claim directly against the "underlying" carrier, bypassing the broker/forwarder in the process.

If a third party broker or forwarder contractually assumed liability, claim may also be filed with that party. However, it should be noted that such a claim does *not* constitute notice to the underlying carrier; should the third party fail to pay, the claimant has no recourse against the carrier unless claim was filed with *it* within the time limit. (Similarly, the filing of a claim with the underlying carrier will not serve as notice to the third party.)

If multiple carriers were involved in the movement of the goods *and* those carriers had—by contractual agreement or statutory mandate—"joint and several" liability for the shipment (*see above*), claim may be filed with either the originating or the delivering carrier.[5] The timely filing of a claim with either such party serves as legal notice to all carriers participating in the movement; thus, if the carrier with whom the claim is filed fails to pay, it may be re-filed with another even if the time limit for such filings has expired. However, where the movement involves three or more carriers, the filing of a claim with a "bridge" carrier—one that neither originated nor delivered the shipment—will *not* serve as notice to any other participating carrier.

Although some carriers and insurors will dispute this, the

---

5 Where rail movements are involved, the "delivering" carrier is deemed to be the last carrier that performed *line-haul* transportation, *not* a carrier that may have performed destination switching service only.

overwhelming body of case law is to the effect that it is immaterial who files the claim. Obviously the party entitled to recover—the owner, or some other party to whom the owner has assigned his rights—will at some stage have to participate actively in the proceedings. But the claim itself may be prepared and filed by anyone, whether consignor, consignee, third party, etc.; legal notice to the carrier is accomplished without regard to the identity of the claimant.

35
Time Limits for Filing Claims

ORDINARILY THE TIME WITHIN WHICH CLAIMS MUST BE FILED will be established contractually. The Interstate Commerce Act, the Warsaw Convention, the Carriage of Goods by Sea Act (COGSA), etc., do set forth some standards, but these merely set a "floor" on the shortest permissible contractual limits; they are *not* "statutes of limitation," in that the parties are free to agree on *longer* times than set forth therein.

In practice, of course, this rarely happens; to the extent that minimum time limits are established by law, they become the *de facto* standard.

For rail and motor common carriage subject to economic regulation by the Interstate Commerce Commission, that limit is nine months, measured from the date of delivery (or, if delivery was not made, the date on which it would ordinarily have been made).

Rail service deregulated by administrative order of the ICC under the provision of the Staggers Rail Act allowing this[1] is also nominally subject to that minimum time limit. However, the Act also allows carriers to offer "alternative" terms of carrier liability, which the carriers have applied liberally by conditioning reduced-rate offerings on shippers' agreeing to lesser claim-filing limits—often as little as four months from delivery.

---

1   49 U.S.C. § 10505.

Interstate domestic surface freight forwarder service, offered to the shipping public as such, is likewise subject to the nine-month minimum for filing claims.[2] But brokers and other third parties who assume in-transit liability for shipments, if offering their service to the public on this basis, are subject to no such constraint (although the underlying rail and motor services they employ, to the extent they are subject to ICC regulation, have no such exemption).

Motor common carriage in intrastate commerce may be subject to varying minimum claim periods—usually nine months from delivery—by state regulatory authorities, to the extent the service is economically regulated by the state in which it is performed.

International air carriage under the Warsaw Convention has by far the shortest time limits for the filing of claims; it is also the only form of transportation for which such time limits ordinarily vary depending on the nature of the claim. Damage claims must be filed within seven days from the date of arrival at the destination airport (*not* the date of ultimate delivery if, as is usual, the shipment has a further surface movement at the end of the air transportation, except where the airline itself undertakes to provide or contract for the surface movement); claims for loss must be filed within 14 days from the same date; and claims for delay must be filed within 120 days after that date. These minima, however, are frequently extended by airline contractual agreement.

In addition, with respect to international air service the claimant does *not* have the legal option of instituting suit in lieu of filing a claim; the timely filing of a claim is required to give the claimant standing to sue.

Strictly speaking, COGSA establishes no minimum time limit on the filing of claims against water carriers. It does, how-

---

2 Freight forwarder economic deregulation, effective December 22, 1986, did not extend to the liability standards of 49 U.S.C. § 11707, which include the nine-month minimum time limit.

TIME LIMITS FOR FILING CLAIMS

ever, specify that claimants must be contractually permitted at least one year from the date of delivery or expected delivery in which to bring suit in court, which clearly renders any contractual claim-filing period of less than that unenforceable. In the usual course of events, carriers will voluntarily agree to an extension of the time limit for lawsuits when they receive a claim.

Other forms of carriage—motor service that is not subject to economic regulation, domestic air service, contract service by all modes, etc.—are governed in this regard only by contractual provisions. If the contract is silent on this question, the time limit is that of the general statute of limitations in the jurisdiction in which suit is or may be brought, which may vary from as little as two to as many as eight years, measured from the date of delivery or expected delivery.

For purposes of whatever time limit applies, a claim is not deemed "filed" until it is *actually in the carrier's hands*. In particular, the postmark date is *not* the date on which the claim is deemed filed; the date that counts is, rather, that on which the carrier receives it.

36
Carrier Processing of Claims

EXCEPT AS TO SURFACE MOTOR AND RAIL CARRIAGE SUBJECT TO regulation by the Interstate Commerce Commission (and, in some states, intrastate carriage regulated by state agencies), there are no rigorous standards for carrier handling of claims filed by shippers.

As to ICC-regulated carriage, regulations[1] require carriers to do the following:

- They must give written acknowledgment of each claim within 30 days of receiving it;
- They must open a separate file on each claim;
- They must investigate all claims "promptly"; and
- They must either dispose of a claim within 120 days of receiving it, or notify the claimant in writing of the status of the claim at the expiration of that period (and there is a requirement for further such notifications at 60-day intervals for so long as the claim remains pending).

As a practical matter, these rules are enforced by the ICC (at least as of early 1989, when this is written) very laxly; they will rarely take action even on direct complaints registered by

---

1 Code of Federal Regulations, 49 CFR Part 1005; carriers are required to incorporate these rules into tariffs filed with the Commission.

claimants.[2] Thus, as with carriers not subject to these standards, the claimant's ultimate recourse against carriers that are dilatory about responding to claims lies in litigation or via the other avenues available when they are dissatisfied with carrier disposition of a claim (*see below*).

"Disposition" of a claim, of course, means (a) payment in full to the claimant; (b) declining the claim in full; or (c) offering a compromise settlement—and for legal purposes the last is considered "disposition" only if it incorporates a specifically stated declination of the claim to the extent that it exceeds the compromise offer.

Strictly speaking, there is no basis in law for compromising claims for loss, damage or delay; as a legal matter the carrier either is or is not liable for a specified or determinable amount of damages, and there is no middle ground. Indeed, to get technical about it, an argument could be made that compromise settlements of loss-and-damage claims constitute unlawful rebates with respect to regulated transportation subject to the so-called "filed rate doctrine" of the law.[3]

However, the author is aware of no court case in which compromise settlements have been successfully challenged on that basis. Compromise is a time-honored way of resolving difficult or uncertain questions without subjecting the parties to the problems and burdens of litigation, and is widely accepted as such in our society.

This is not, of course, to suggest that every claim is a suitable candidate for compromise; if carrier liability is clearly established (or shown not to exist) by the facts of a particular

---

[2] An exception exists with respect to household goods carriers due to the political sensitivity of this form of carriage (because shippers are mainly individual consumers); the ICC is fairly zealous about dealing with complaints of slow or improper claims handling by such carriers.

[3] Incorporated in the Interstate Commerce Act as 49 U.S.C. § 10762(a), which requires carriers to collect, and shippers to pay, no more and no less than the rates and charges set forth in published and effective tariffs on file with the ICC.

case, neither party should permit itself to be pressured into unjustified compromises. But where there exists reasonable doubt on the question of liability—or where considerations of equity may induce one party or the other to surrender a portion of his rights under strict application of the law—compromise is a valid and viable approach that should not be scorned by either.

Indeed, an unreasonable unwillingness to compromise is probably responsible for more disruptions in shipper-carrier relations than any other single factor. The author was once asked to arbitrate a claims dispute between a shipper and carrier that had grown so acrimonious that, according to the parties themselves, it imperiled a relationship between them that had endured for years; each believed so strongly that it had the right of the matter that both were unwilling to give way an inch.

The amount in dispute?—$27.00.

37

Litigating Claims Disputes

ONE OF THE MOST JEALOUSLY GUARDED OF AMERICANS' CONSTItutional rights is that of free access to the courts to resolve private disputes. As in other areas, the dissatisfied claimant is entitled to take his case against the carrier into court.

Court action must be initiated within specified time limits, usually (although not always—*see below*) measured from the date on which the carrier declines the claim, in part or in full. Such declinations must be set forth by the carrier in writing, in clear and unambiguous terms;[1] but even if claimant and carrier continue to discuss the claim after that, the legal clock keeps on ticking unless the carrier leads the shipper to believe the declination is withdrawn and the claim reopened for further consideration. As a general rule, the claimant will be wise to consider the original date of declination binding under virtually any cir-

---

1   Standards for carrier declinations are formally set forth in the Interstate Commerce Act (49 U.S.C. § 11707(e)), which also provides that (a) offers of compromise are not to be construed as declinations unless the carrier specifically says so and offers reasons therefor, and (b) insurance-company communiques are likewise not declinations unless the insurance company so states, offers reasons therefor, *and* states expressly that it is acting on behalf of the carrier. In general this is merely a codification of standards of common law applicable to forms and modes of carriage not subject to the IC Act; however, claimants should be wary of any correspondence from carriers not regulated by the ICC which a court might construe, under less rigorous non-statutory standards, as declinations.

cumstances, and to initiate any litigation within the specified time after that date even if discussions about the claim are still in progress.

Litigation is also a viable option if the claimant is dissatisfied with the carrier's handling of the claim for other reasons, such as, for example, dilatory handling by the carrier. As already discussed *(see above)*, carriers do not always comply with regulations requiring them to process claims promptly; and some carriers are not even bound by such rules.

Indeed, a claimant may even take his case to court when the carrier agrees to pay his claim in full, if he wants to amend it to ask for a higher amount. However, if the claimant *accepts* a proffered payment (whether as a compromise or in the full amount of the original claim), he will almost always be required to sign a "release"—either a separate document or simply a statement in the endorsement block on the back of the check itself—relieving the carrier from further liability. Although there are very limited exceptions to this rule, the signing of such a release will generally *estop* the claimant from recovering additional damages later, in court or otherwise, *even if evidence of such further damages does not emerge until after the payment is made and the release executed.* Claimants should therefore be certain they have incorporated their *entire* economic loss in the claim before accepting a settlement, since under the law they are unlikely to have a second chance.

The litigatory time limits are, as with those governing the filing of claims, for the most part contractual in nature. If the contract is silent as to the time for filing lawsuits, the pertinent general statute of limitations (which varies, depending on jurisdiction, between as few as two and as many as eight years) applies. However, where common (*not* contract) carriage is involved, the law establishes certain minima:

- For railroads, at least two years and a day following the date of declination must be allowed.[2]

LITIGATING CLAIMS DISPUTES

- For *ICC-regulated* motor carriage, the two-years-and-a-day minimum likewise governs. Strictly speaking, it is the nature of the individual shipment in question that determines whether the carriage is or is not subject to regulation (and hence to this minimum time limit on filing suit); if it is not subject to regulatory jurisdiction, it is irrelevant that the carrier may *also* provide regulated transportation. However, many motor carriers employ standard-form bills of lading, which specify this time period and are thus binding on the parties, for both their regulated and their unregulated service.
- For international air carriage, the Warsaw Convention also provides a two-year time limit, but measured from arrival of the shipment at the destination airport. Additionally, whereas claimants may bring suit against other types of carriers in lieu of filing a claim (provided they do so within the time limit for filing claims, *not* that for suing), the claimant's right to sue an airline with regard to an international shipment is contingent on his prior timely filing of a claim. Some domestic carriers follow this general standard for domestic air freight, others have their own standard contractual provisions.
- As already discussed (*see above*), the statutory minimum time limit under COGSA for suing a water carrier is one year from the date of delivery of the shipment (or, if delivery wasn't made, expected delivery); however, carriers will ordinarily agree to an extension of this period if claim is filed before it expires.

---

2   This applies both to interstate and foreign commerce and, by dint of the Staggers Rail Act provision obliging states to follow Federal standards in regulating rail service within their own borders, to intrastate carriage as well. Where rail service has been administratively deregulated by the Interstate Commerce Commission, the law (49 U.S.C. § 10505(e)) requires carriers to adhere to statutory standards as regards questions of loss and damage and carrier liability, including the two-years-and-a-day minimum time for filing suit; but it does allow carriers to offer "alternative terms," which may include a shorter time for suing and which, if the shipper accepts them in exchange for a reduced level of rates, are legally binding.

With regard to contract or unregulated common carriage, there are no statutory "floors" on the time limit for filing suit; and some carriers utilize standard-form contracts or bills of lading which provide extraordinarily short periods. Shippers should familiarize themselves with the terms of all such contractual agreements.

As the suing party, the claimant will ordinarily have the choice of "venue"—that is, he may bring suit before the court of his choice, provided only that the court has litigatory jurisdiction in the matter under the ordinary standards governing this area.[3] It will thus ordinarily be possible for the claimant to bring his suit in a court located at or near his place of business (although there are occasional exceptions).

Litigation will normally be a cumbersome, costly and time-consuming option, and accordingly may be impractical except where unusually large sums are involved or where a "test case" is sought to govern disposition of other, similar claims. For the most part, thus, it will not be a suitable means of resolving claims problems.

One alternative that is frequently overlooked, however, is that of filing suit in small-claims court. Such courts have been established in every state for the precise purpose of handling disputes in equity that do not involve sums large enough to otherwise warrant the cost of litigation; they provide an avenue for low-cost and speedy (if somewhat rough-hewn) justice. They are often used to settle consumer and private-grievance cases, as popularized by television's *People's Court*; but they are also available to business enterprises on the same basis. Small-claims courts have limits on the dollar value of disputes they will entertain, ranging from under $1,000 to as much as several thousand dollars, depending on the state. Filing procedures are

---

3 Certain limitations apply as to railroads under the Staggers Rail Act (49 U.S.C. § 11707(d)(2) and as to international air carriers under the Warsaw Convention. In addition, under Admiralty law suit involving ocean carriage may be brought against the vessel itself *in rem* in Admiralty court in any port where the vessel may be found.

greatly simplified, costs are minimal, procedures are quite informal, and cases proceed in rapid-fire succession. Individuals may, and commonly do, represent themselves before such courts rather than engaging an attorney; corporations must be represented by legal counsel under the law, although courts will sometimes allow non-attorney managers to provide representation if the other party raises no objection.

The drawback of small-claims courts is that judges will almost always lack detailed knowledge of or experience in freight transportation in general, and questions involving in-transit loss, damage or delay in particular; and the speed with which such hearings progress allows little unraveling of complex issues. Nevertheless, where a small-claims court is the only economically practical forum available, it should certainly not be ignored.

38
Evidence and the 'Burden of Proof'

THE EVIDENTIARY SLATE IS BLANK WHEN THE PARTIES FIRST walk into court; no fact has been shown yet, nothing has been proved or disproved. The purpose of the hearing or trial is to fill up that slate with information material to the dispute at hand.

In order to structure the orderly development of that information, the law imposes a standard called the "burden of proof" —like a pointer that shifts from one party to the other and indicates which must go forward with presenting evidence. The party bearing the burden of proof at a particular moment is on notice that, unless it can discharge that burden with probative (legally admissible) evidence, it will lose its case *automatically*, even if the other side fails to present any evidence either.

These rigid standards apply formally, of course, only in courts of law. But because the courtroom is, in our society, the ultimate recourse of any party, the same approach tends to spill over, albeit more loosely, into disputes that are not the subject of litigation—not yet, at any rate. Thus, investigation and disposition of claims for freight loss, damage and delay roughly parallel the lines the law prescribes, including particularly this question of burden of proof.

At the outset the burden of proof always rests, in law, on the party making the complaint and claiming economic reparation for injuries it has allegedly suffered at the hands of the other—in the case of L&D claims, the claimant. He bears the threefold burden of proving that:

- at origin the carrier was tendered goods of a certain kind and quantity, in a certain condition, at a certain time; and
- at destination the carrier failed to deliver the same goods in the same quantity and/or the same condition, or made delivery unreasonably late in light of the time when it received them from the shipper; and
- as a result thereof, he (the claimant) incurred economic injury amounting to a specific sum of money.

If the claimant fails to prove even one of these three elements, the matter is ended right there. The proof need not be overwhelming, or even extraordinarily strong (*see below*); but there must be *some* evidence to overcome the legal presumption that, in the absence of proof to the contrary, these things are in fact not true.

Once the claimant has discharged its burden of proof, and thereby made out a *prima facie* (at first glance) case of carrier liability for the claimed damages, "the burden [of proof] shifts to the carrier and remains there."[1] That is, the judicial pointer now moves to the carrier and will never swing back; it will henceforward be the obligation of the carrier to prove somehow that it is not liable, or that it is liable but for a lesser sum than that claimed.

In actuality this is a simplification that, although much beloved of lawyers (and true as a technical matter of law), is not always accurate as a pragmatic description of the situation. The carrier is entitled to rebut any evidence presented by the claimant with evidence of its own; if it succeeds thereby in refuting or neutralizing the claimant's proof on any of these three

---

1   *Super Service Motor Freight Co. v. U.S.*, 350 F.2d 541. One of the leading cases on this point, which is frequently cited, is *Mo. Pac. R. Co. v. Elmore & Stahl*, 337 U.S. 134, reh. den. 377 U.S. 948, decided by the U.S. Supreme Court, commonly called the "Elmore & Stahl" case.

points, as a practical matter the pointer will swing back to the claimant, who must take up cudgels anew in an effort to *successfully* meet its burden.

Assuming the claimant is successful, however, it is now incumbent on the carrier to prove, first, that the complained-of loss, damage or delay was due to one of the "excepted causes" for which it is not liable (*see above*), *and* (b) that it, the carrier, did not contribute in any way to the problem by its own negligence. *Both* things must be proved; the carrier's failure on either count is automatically fatal to its cause notwithstanding an absence of evidence to the contrary. That is, there's now a legal presumption that the loss/damage/delay was *not* due to an excepted cause and that the carrier's negligence *did* contribute to or cause the problem, and it's up to the carrier to prove otherwise.

And, of course, the claimant will have the opportunity to rebut the carrier's presentation with contravening evidence of its own. Thus, while in the technicalities of the law the burden-of-proof pointer may shift only once, as a practical matter it may oscillate back and forth several times as the parties in turn challenge one another's evidence.

Furthermore, in a courtroom the parties are obliged to present their evidence in a structured manner, in order to prevent hearings from dragging on and disrupting judicial functioning; a party that fails to present evidence at the proper time may find that it has thereby forfeited its legal right to present that evidence at all. In the give and take of commercial claims practice, however, there are no such limitations, and any party is free to bring up entirely new evidence at any time.

The concept of the burden of proof must be regarded in the context of the *standard* of proof that will be required—both in court and therefore, as a practical matter, in support of a claim or its declination. *How much* proof, that is, must a party present before it may consider its burden fairly discharged?

In law there are three basic standards of proof employed, depending on the type of case involved and the potential consequences of losing it. Most readers of mystery novels, viewers of televised or cinematic courtroom dramas, etc., will be familiar with the most stringent of these standards, proof "beyond a reasonable doubt"; that is, if the defendant merely casts doubt on the evidence presented against him, notwithstanding that the probability of his guilt appears high, he is exonerated. But this rigorous standard is reserved for cases in criminal law where the defendant faces judicial deprivation of life, liberty or property in punishment for his misconduct, and has no bearing on L&D claim cases.

A second standard of proof is that of "clear and convincing evidence." Under this standard a probability will suffice to decide the case against the defendant, notwithstanding that there may remain some element of unresolved doubt, but the probability must be quite high. This is employed in civil cases in which the defendant faces punitive forfeiture of property rights due to violations of the law, and is likewise inapplicable to cases involving freight claims.

It is the third and least of the standards of legal proof—that of a "preponderance of the evidence"—that prevails in cases in equity, the category in which claims disputes fall. That is, the parties are deemed to start off on a level footing, and whichever can back its position with the most, and most persuasive, evidence will prevail, even if the difference is too slight to be "beyond a reasonable doubt" or even "clear and convincing."

Naturally, such cases involve the greatest scope of juridical discretion. Virtually everyone will be able to identify when doubt exists on a point and when it doesn't, and to assess the reasonableness of the doubt. Most people will also have little difficulty identifying when evidence is, and when it isn't, clear and convincing. But when the decision hangs on evaluation of closely weighted evidentiary presentations involving uncertainties and unresolved contradictions, human predilections and predispositions tend to play a much stronger role; two equally rational individuals might reasonably reach diametrically opposite conclusions (each by a narrow margin) in such a case.

Thus, it behooves each party to assemble, insofar as it can, the strongest possible body of evidence in support of its position, in order to tip the scales as much as possible in its direction. Technical considerations of the law will ordinarily be secondary in freight loss/damage/delay cases; the outcome will most commonly depend rather on the facts of the matter, and the parties' respective abilities to prove those facts. And this holds true both in court and out of it.

At the most basic level, evidence consists of the shipping papers and ancillary documents. The bill of lading and (if separate) delivery receipt will provide *prima facie* proof of a variety of things, including the existence of a shipper-carrier contract, routing, pickup and delivery dates, special handling and protective-service instructions (if any), identity of the party(ies) performing loading and unloading, consist and nature of the shipment itself, apparent condition of the shipment at origin and destination, limitation of carrier's liability (if any), special-damages notations, etc. If a separate shipment manifest was prepared, it may provide supplemental information in some of these areas. As to shipments moving pursuant to contracts of sale, the shipper's invoice will be evidence of the amount of damages incurred by the claimant. Driver or pilot logs may serve to identify unusual occurrences in the transportation of motor or air shipments.

The nature of *prima facie* evidence, however, is that it is subject to rebuttal; thus, what the bill of lading (or any other document) may show is not necessarily determinative in most of the areas identified if there is other, more persuasive evidence to the contrary.[2] The documents, that is, are for most purposes indicators of the facts rather than being facts in themselves; and

---

2   A limited exception must be noted for contractual matters such as released-value and special-damages notations, which in general must, as a matter of law, be shown on the bill of lading itself (*see discussions of these questions elsewhere*); but even in these instances there are some circumstances in which the presence or absence of such contractual elements will not necessarily be conclusive.

if those indicators are proved false, it will be the facts as they are otherwise shown to exist that will govern.

Both shippers and carriers tend to rely too heavily on such documents, especially as to count and condition of the shipment at origin and destination. A clear delivery receipt (no notation of shortage or damage), for example, does not bar claims if it is shown by other evidence not to reflect the facts. A carrier's acceptance of origin count of the shipment does not necessarily establish the accuracy of the count if there is other, contradictory evidence. And so forth. It is the *totality* of the picture, rather than any single evidentiary element, that controls on most questions.

Accordingly, where any dispute exists the claimant should try to bolster the evidence of the documents by supplemental proof to the extent possible. This may include the testimony of dock personnel, inspectors and repair technicians, packaging designers, etc.; photographs depicting the condition of the goods, the carrier's equipment and the like; results of examinations or quality-control tests of the goods themselves; records of past, similar shipments (to establish a salient difference from the shipment to which the claim pertains); and so on.

In some cases shippers will use instruments or devices to monitor the condition of the shipment in transit; typical are impact recorders or triggers which indicate the "G"-forces[3] to which the shipment was subjected, and thermal recorders to indicate temperatures to which it was exposed. Records developed by such equipment may prove valuable; however, the shipper should be prepared to support the accuracy of both the class and type of instrument/device used and the particular unit(s) itself (themselves), both in court and (if the carrier raises the question) as part of the claims process. In addition, impact-recorder records

---

3 A "G"-force is equal to the acceleration imparted by the force of gravity at the Earth's surface, *i.e.*, 32 feet/sec.^{2}

must be compared to a benchmark based on past, similar shipments to carry much weight.

Some events and occurrences may be evidence in and of themselves, independent of any interpretation or explanation, under the legal doctrine of *res ipsa loquitor* (loosely, "the thing speaks for itself"). A broken or missing seal on a truck or railcar door, for example, is mute testimony to the probability that the door was opened at some point (for that reason both carrier and shipper should keep seal records meticulously). Holes in the floor, sides or roof of carrier equipment, broken weather-stripping around doors, etc., suggest how water or detritus may have entered the vehicle. The absence of dunnage may indicate improper loading, as may the load's having shifted in transit in some circumstances. Indeed, the mere fact that loss or damage occurred may be the strongest available evidence of what actually happened.

Sometimes a little elementary detective work will uncover additional evidence of value. A comparison of scale weights, for example, may resolve uncertainties about count when shipments are allegedly delivered incomplete. Meteorological records may show whether precipitation could be responsible for water damage. Results of official accident investigations may be of consequence in some instances. Trip manifests or warehouse/terminal inventory records may help locate possible sources of contamination.

Assembling all this evidence, or even a significant proportion, would obviously be a formidable task. It should be obvious, however, that not all of these evidentiary elements will apply to any given claim. Furthermore, evidence will be of importance only as to such issues as are in dispute; that is, if the other side doesn't argue a particular point only a small amount of evidence will be required to prove it—or, if there is a "stipulation" (formal acknowledgment or agreement) on the point, no evidence at all. Thus, as a rule the evidentiary burden on both parties will be readily manageable as the disagreement centers on just one or two key matters.

Particular attention should be focused on the question of negligence as it pertains to L&D claims. As noted, the claimant is not obliged to prove the carrier to have been negligent; rather, once its (the claimant's) initial burden of proof has been discharged a presumption is created that the carrier *was* negligent, and it is legally up to the carrier to prove otherwise.

Construed rigorously, this burden of "proving a negative" would be all but impossible to discharge, obliging the carrier to account for and justify its actions literally moment by moment for the entire time it had custody of the goods. The courts take a more practical view, however, and the carrier will ordinarily satisfy this requirement merely by providing general evidence that it handled the goods in unexceptional fashion and that there were no untoward events during its custodianship that resulted from factors within its (or its employees' or agents') control. Even so, such evidence must be presented; the law will not presume the carrier to have been non-negligent in the absence of any effort by it to speak to this point.

Clearly, it is incumbent on the parties to be aware of their respective burdens of proof at all stages of the claims process, including particularly the investigatory phase of the case when evidence is being assembled. No case has ever been lost by the assemblage of *too much* evidence, but a great many have been lost, notwithstanding their apparent or actual merit, by inadequate attention to this vital area.

39
Arbitration

IN OUR SOCIETY ANY PARTY HAS THE LEGAL RIGHT TO GO TO court; but he also has the option of waiving that right in favor of submitting a dispute to someone else for less formalistic arbitration.[1]

The disadvantage of such extra-legal arbitration is, of course, that it deprives the parties of many legal rights and protections of which they might avail themselves in court. For example, the right of "discovery"—compelling one's litigatory adversary to disgorge evidence in its possession that supports one's own case—will ordinarily not be available in arbitration; the legal rules of evidence are generally relaxed to some degree; and in general there is less attention paid to the technical aspects of the law in both the hearing and the decision of the arbitrator.

This lower degree of attention to technicalities may, however, be a benefit as well as a drawback. Not only does it tend to greatly expedite proceedings, but it may allow the parties to

---

1 Parties are not, of course, required to give up any of their rights to legal redress in order to avail themselves of arbitration. As a general rule, however, arbitration will be most useful if it is to at least some degree binding—that is, involves some agreement between the parties to waive or restrict their rights to go to court, which thereby requires or encourages them to accept the decision of the arbitrator rather than merely reargue the matter in another forum whenever they're dissatisfied with the result. After all, there's not much benefit to arbitration if it's merely going to be a prologue to the litigation for which it's intended to substitute.

dispense with the high-cost services of legal counsel—required in court—in prosecuting or defending the cases.[2]

Another advantage is that arbitration avoids the often-lengthy delays occasioned by today's overcrowded court dockets. In some jurisdictions it may take many months, even a year or more, to secure a court hearing in an equity case, and "continuances"—postponements—may in some circumstances drag the case on for much longer.

Arbitration requires the consent of both parties. This may be given either on an *ad hoc* basis—*i.e.*, case by case—or as part of a broader contractual agreement. Some shipper-carrier contracts, for example, have special dispute-settlement clauses committing both parties to submission of disputes to arbitration.

Such an agreement must also identify the arbitrator(s) or provide a clear basis for his (their) selection. In some instances a particular individual, generally a recognized expert in the field, will be identified;[3] in others there will be provision only for mutual agreement on an individual or panel of arbitrators. One often-used approach is for each disputant to choose one arbitrator and for the two chosen individuals to mutually select a third person to join them on a three-member panel.

There are a few standing forums for arbitration of L&D claims disputes. The Association of American Railroads, for example, has established such a program in conjunction with the American Arbitration Association for the resolution of claims disputes involving rail shipments. The motor-carrier-sponsored National Freight Claim Council and the Shippers National Freight Claim Council have jointly created the Transportation Arbitration Board, which makes use of professional claims managers as arbitrators.

---

2 Even so, any party, whether claimant or carrier, should think twice at the least before seeking to represent his own interests before an arbitrator as much as in open court (*see above*).

3 The author, for example, maintains an arbitration program for claims and other transportation disputes.

ARBITRATION

By far the most comprehensive such program is that maintained by the American Movers Conference for household goods carriers and their shippers. This program has special status conferred by the Household Goods Transportation Act of 1980, which virtually directed its establishment; this statute specifies that carriers who don't maintain or participate in an arbitration program will be liable for legal fees incurred by claimants who successfully prosecute their actions in court. Although not required to handle claims disputes through this program, claimants, too, have statutory encouragement to do so in the form of a provision of the act that lets carriers recover their own legal costs if they successfully defend a lawsuit that's found to be "frivolous"—*i.e.*, unwarranted by the facts.

The act imposes a number of standards on household goods arbitration programs, including requirements that sharply limit the maximum arbitration charge (and make it refundable if the claimant is successful) and make prompt decisions mandatory. Carriers are obliged to notify all shippers of the existence of the program, and to make proper forms available. The claimant (although not the carrier) is free to contest an arbitration ruling in court; but if it loses it may be, again, obliged to pay the carrier's legal costs.

40
Insurance

UNDER RULES MAINTAINED BY THE INTERSTATE COMMERCE COMmission,[1] common motor carriers subject to the Commission's jurisdiction must maintain cargo insurance "for the protection of the public [*i.e.*, shippers]"; ICC-regulated brokers must maintain surety bonds.

The amounts involved are comparatively small; truckers' cargo insurance must be only $5,000 "for loss of or damage to property carried on any one motor vehicle" and $10,000 "for loss of or damage to or aggregated of losses or damages of or to property occurring at any one time and place," and the broker bond is for only $10,000. Moreover, when insurance costs escalated sharply in the mid-1980's the ICC sharply relaxed standards for motor carriers and brokers to "self-insure," relieving them of the obligation to buy such coverage.

Nevertheless, in some instances the existence of such insurance or bond may offer claimants an avenue to collect, within the limits of the coverage, when a carrier is unwilling or unable to pay a "perfected" claim. That is, the claimant may file his claim directly with the insurance company or bonding agent.

To qualify as "perfected," either (a) the carrier or broker must have admitted liability in a particular amount (and even then the insuror or bonding agent is free to disagree), or (b) the claimant must have obtained a legal judgment against it. Even then, the insurance company will be liable only within the limits

---

[1] Code of Federal Regulations, 49 CFR Part 1043.

of its coverage on a per-claim basis; and bonding agents are liable only for an *aggregate* of the $10,000 bond, which will have to be pro-rated among all valid claimants if the total amount of their claims exceeds that sum.

It is important to distinguish this ICC-mandated insurance and bonds from other insurance coverage maintained by the carrier or broker for its own protection. Many carriers, for instance, also carry insurance against high-dollar claims, intended to protect them against catastrophic losses. This type of insurance may be claimed against only by the carrier itself, and payments will go only to it (less what is often quite a high deductible). The regulation-required insurance and bonds, on the other hand, is payable only to claimants who are unable to collect from the carrier (and is subject to no deductible).

Payments under insurance or bond claims do not legally relieve the carrier or broker from its obligation to make up any difference between the payment and the full value of the claim.

41
'Self-Help'

ONE OF THE MOST CONTROVERSIAL AREAS IN THE ENTIRE FIELD of freight loss and damage claims is that of claimant "self-help," also familiarly known as "set-off"—that is, unilateral deduction by the claimant of the amount of an unpaid claim (in whole or in part) from money otherwise owed by it to the carrier, usually freight charges.

The author must accept a considerable part of the responsibility for arousing this controversy. Back in 1977-78, in the "Questions & Answers" column in *Traffic World* magazine, he wrote a series of discussions of this subject and arrived at a conclusion diametrically opposed to the "conventional wisdom" of the transportation industry—to wit, that set-offs of this nature are legally valid provided the claim itself is valid. To this date most other authorities in this field—including the (motor carriers') National Freight Claim Council, the Shippers National Freight Claim Council, and the Interstate Commerce Commission, among others—have continued to disagree with the author's position to at least some degree (although their stances, too, differ somewhat from one another).

It remains the author's view that there is clear ratification for this type of set-off to be found in the case law propounded by the courts (including the U.S. Supreme Court). However, the ensuing discussion must be read with an awareness of the disagreements it has evoked.

At the outset it is critical to recognize that *"set-off" may not legally take the place of filing a claim*; that is, the claimant may not simply deduct, from payments he owes the carrier, money he contends is owed to him in compensation for cargo loss, damage or delay in lieu of formally claiming that money. If he does so he almost assuredly forfeits his right to recover, and may place himself in violation of legal standards requiring him to pay carrier freight charges.

As already discussed (*see above*), the timely filing of a formal claim is a legal prerequisite to any recovery by the claimant. If the applicable time limit is allowed to expire within a claim being filed, nothing will ordinarily serve to resurrect it and the claimant will lose all entitlement to any recovery *no matter what the merits of the claim itself*. Thus, shippers who employ immediate set-off as a substitute for filing claims face the risk that the carrier may simply wait for the time limit for filing the claim to expire and then sue for recovery of the unpaid freight charges; the time-barred claim will not be admissible as a defense in such a suit.

Furthermore, where transportation subject to the Interstate Commerce Act is involved, the shipper subjects itself to civil or even criminal penalties under the so-called Elkins Act,[1] which prohibits shippers from "solicit[ing], accept[ing] or receiv[ing]" rebates or concessions or otherwise securing transportation at less than a carrier's legally published tariff rate. As this is written (early 1989), the Elkins Act is but lightly enforced; nevertheless, it remains on the books and may be invoked against shippers who cannot properly support set-offs of unpaid claims against freight charges they owe to ICC-regulated carriers.

The question of set-off more properly arises when the claimant has complied with the claims-filing requirement on a timely basis but has failed to secure payment of the claim. Some shippers give the carrier but a short time in which to respond to a claim before initiating set-off; some, in fact, wait not at all but

---

1   The provisions of this formerly separate statute are now incorporated in the Interstate Commerce Act (esp. 49 U.S.C. §§ 11902-11904).

set off coincident with the filing of the claim. As a commercial practice this is scarcely very reasonable and is likely to do injury to the company's relations with its transportation suppliers; the author does *not* mean to recommend or condone such discourtesy (at least) under any but the most extreme circumstances.[2] But as a legal matter, the right of set-off exists, contingent on the validity of the claim, onward from the moment the claim has been properly and timely filed.

It is possible that the act of set-off will itself end the matter; the carrier will accept the situation and that will be that. However, the claimant must be prepared in such cases for the carrier to file suit to recover its unpaid freight charges, and must be in a position to defend its action by proving the validity of its claim.

Strictly speaking, the Interstate Commerce Act requires that the freight charges of carriers subject to its jurisdiction be paid in money and not otherwise. This requirement, which has been invoked in past cases to forbid various types of "barter" arrangements (such as exchanges of services between shippers and carriers), is cited by those who contend that set-off of claims amounts against unpaid freight charges is not legal. (Note, however, that there is no comparable standard applicable to service not subject to the IC Act, and therefore this argument is not relevant when applied to their situations.)

However, it is also a common-law right of any creditor "to apply the unappropriated monies of his debtor, in his hands, in extinguishment of the debts due to him."[3] That is, one who owes money to someone but is also owed money by the same person may unilaterally discharge the debt he is owed by deducting it from the amount he owes; the law does not require a useless exchange of checks between the parties. And since it is monetary

---

2   Exceptions might arise where the claimant had reason to doubt the carrier's continued solvency (and ability to pay the claim), or had past experience with extreme dilatory tactics by the carrier in handling claims, etc.—that is, where it believed its recovery might be jeopardized by delay in acting. (*Also see below.*)

3   See *U.S. v. Munsey Trust Co.*, 332 U.S. 234, 239.

indebtedness that is in question on both sides, there is no violation of the payment-in-money requirement of the IC Act.

Thus, if sued by the carrier against whose freight bills he has set off unpaid claims, the claimant's defense is that he has indeed paid those freight bills by waiving or foregoing his independent prosecution of his claims.

If the claim has already been "liquidated" by means of a court judgment in the claimant's favor, the case would seem to be altogether clear-cut; even some of the authorities who otherwise disagree with the legality of such set-off accept its validity in these circumstances.[4] The claimant need merely present the court judgment affirming its right to the money and the case will be concluded.

If the claim is not liquidated, it may nevertheless be raised as a defense against the carrier's collection action. Provided the claim itself was timely filed, securing the claimant's right to recovery, this defense is not barred *even if the time for the claimant to initiate a lawsuit of its own has expired*. The courts have repeatedly declined to construe statutes of limitation as precluding parties from raising particular issues in their defense even if the right to raise those issues *ab initio* in court no longer exists.[5]

And if the claim is found valid, the court will in effect ratify the set-off by leaving the parties as it found them, with no

---

4   The Shippers National Freight Claim Council has expressly stated its agreement with this limited position, and the (motor carriers') National Freight Claim Council appears to be in less enthusiastic accord as well. The ICC, however, remains adamantly opposed to *any* form of set-off, according to its most recent pronouncement on the subject (Administrative Ruling No. 128, March 9, 1978); its view is that the two transactions payment of freight charges and payment of the claim—must be entirely separate and independent.

5   "If [the] litigation is not stale [*i.e.*, if the carrier's suit to collect its freight charges is not time-barred], then no issue in it can be deemed stale." *U.S. v. Western Pac. R. Co.*, 352 U.S. 59, 72.

monetary award to the carrier.[6] In other words, as a popular sports phrasing goes, "no harm, no foul"—although the set-off of an unliquidated claim *might* be construed as a technical violation of the IC Act (even this is far from clear), there will be no adverse consequences to the claimant.

On the other hand, if the claim is *not* upheld in court—that is, if the claimant loses on this issue—not only is the set-off invalidated and the claimant required to pay the withheld freight charges with interest, but he faces possible prosecution for violations of the Elkins Act (*see above*).

It is important to note that the claimant may not "have his cake and eat it too" in selecting his remedy for unpaid claims. He has the right to take his case to court; *or* he may (if fully persuaded of the validity of his position) exercise set-off; but he is ill-advised indeed to do both. A claim that is *sub judice* (under consideration) in one court may not be raised as a defense in another; that would obviously give rise to the possibility of two different decisions by two different courts on the same case, and will not be countenanced by the law. Hence, the set-off will not be validated if the carrier sues for recovery of its withheld freight charges while the claimant is also suing on its claim (except in the unlikely event that both suits are before the same court and may therefore be consolidated).[7]

Once again, the author wishes to warn that the foregoing represents to a considerable extent his own construction of the case law and is in disagreement with the views of others. However, diligent legal researches have failed to uncover even a

---

6 *North Chicago Rolling Mill Co. v. Ore & Steel Co.*, 152 U.S. 576; *C. & N. W. Ry. Co. v. Lindell*, 281 U.S. 14; *Burlington Northern Inc. v. U.S.*, 462 F.2d 526; *Johnson Motor Transp. v. U.S.*, 149 F.Supp. 175; *N. P. Ry. Co. v. Associated General Contractors of N.D.*, 152 F.Supp. 126.

7 *Akers Motor Lines, Inc. v. Lady Cornell Comb Co., Inc.*, 203 F.Supp. 156.

single court case that would seem to refute the views expressed here, so the author feels comfortable in offering this discussion here.

At the same time, in light of the controversy surrounding this question (not to mention the potential penalties for improper exercise), it should be obvious that set-off is not a right to be exercised lightly by any claimant. It should be reserved only for circumstances where collection of claims poses a serious real-world problem, and the author strongly advises that any claimant secure legal advice on a case-by-case basis before taking such a step.

42
Claims Against Bankrupt Carriers

THE MARKET TURMOIL THAT FOLLOWED TRANSPORTATION REGulation (and is still going on in early 1989 as these words are written) has engendered an historically unprecedented number of bankruptcies among carriers—especially, though by no means exclusively, motor carriers.

Realistically, anyone with unpaid freight loss-and-damage claims against a bankrupt carrier stands little chance of collecting much money. He must queue up with other creditors of the bankrupt's estate, many of whom are likely to have higher-priority (under bankruptcy law) rights to whatever assets the estate may have, and will be lucky if he receives even a few cents on the dollar.

Accordingly, where possible a claimant should take other measures to recover unpaid claims in such circumstances. *Claims should still be filed*, in order to preserve the claimant's rights (*see above*); but the claimant must look actively to ways of recovering his money other than simply waiting for payment from the bankrupt.

One alternative, of course, is set-off against any monies, such as freight charges, still owing *to* the carrier. Although the legal status of the set-off is still dependent, as with non-bankrupt carriers, on the validity of the claim (*see above*), the likelihood of prosecution for Elkins Act violations in such circumstances may be regarded as extremely small; moreover, it should be obvious that a bankrupt carrier is scarcely well-positioned to contest a claim in court.

Not only may pre-bankruptcy claims be set off against debts to the carrier that arose prior to the date of bankruptcy, but if the carrier continues to operate after that date (under court supervision) post-bankruptcy freight charges, too, may be levied by the claimant. This is particularly important, since it affords the claimant an opportunity to secure the equivalent of "in-kind" payment of claims on which he would otherwise have little hope of any recovery. However, it should be emphasized that the reverse does *not* hold true; that is, claims arising out of the carrier's continued post-bankruptcy operations may not be set off against pre-bankruptcy debts.[1]

In some instances bankrupt carriers' cargo insurors have formally notified all known claimants to exercise their set-off rights. Even those who disagree with set-off in other areas acknowledge that insurors of bankrupt carriers may require claimants to set off claims against unpaid pre-bankruptcy freight charges; and it is established in law that failure by the claimant to make such set-off will invalidate its claim against the insurance company, although a claim will still exist, for whatever it may be worth, against the estate of the bankrupt itself.[2]

Thus, a claimant who receives such a communication from an insuror and nevertheless, *after* that, makes any payment to the carrier may expect to have the amount of that payment deducted from his claim before the insurance company will consider it. Except to that extent, however, insurors of ICC-regulated motor carriers are obliged to honor claims against the bankrupt up to the full value of their mandated coverage.

---

1   This is less troublesome than might be expected, since court supervision of the post-bankruptcy operations makes it likely that valid claims arising therefrom will be paid promptly.
2   *In Re Yale Express System, Inc.*, 362 F.2d 111. This is the one exception made by the ICC in its adamant denunciation of set-off practices in its Administrative Ruling No. 128, dated March 9, 1978.

A much-publicized feature of motor carrier bankruptcies in recent years has been their spawning of balance due billings to shippers based on the so-called "filed rate doctrine" of the law.[3] Competitive pressures of the deregulated market have encouraged many carriers to bill for their service at less than tariff rates, a practice that understandably is especially prevalent among those nearing the brink of insolvency. When such a carrier declares bankruptcy, it is now routine that an independent auditor will be engaged to review its past billings and collect undercharges from shippers based strictly on published tariffs.

Leaving aside both the equities of this situation and the availability of legal defenses,[4] the shipper retains the right to deduct unpaid pre-bankruptcy claims from any such balance due payments. This right is the same whether the bankrupt's estate has retained title to the proceeds of such balance due billings or has "sold" that right to an independent audit/collection agency; clearly, the estate cannot sell any greater entitlement than it itself possesses, and its entitlement is only to the *net* (if any) balance due after claims indebtedness is deducted. Finally, if the claim arose out of interline service as to which the participating carriers assumed "joint and several liability" (*see above*), it may be re-filed with another participant. Both the origin and the delivering line-haul carrier are individually liable to the claimant for loss, damage or delay that occurred at *any* juncture during the course of the movement (irrespective of the identity of the carrier that had actual possession of the shipment at the time the loss, damage or delay occurred); and "bridge" carriers are liable for any loss, damage or delay that took place while the goods were in their custody.

---

3 49 U.S.C. § 10761(a), which requires carriers to charge for transportation service, and shippers to pay, based strictly on rates and charges set forth in tariffs the carrier has duly published and filed with the Interstate Commerce Commission.

4 See the author's *What to Do When You're Dunned for Undercharges* (Great Falls, VA: Barrett Transportation Consultants, 2nd ed., 1988).

MANAGER'S GUIDE TO CLAIMS

As previously discussed (*see above*), it's irrelevant whether re-filing of the claim with an interline carrier occurs before or after expiration of the time limit for filing claims, providing the *original* claim was timely filed with the bankrupt carrier. In such cases the courts have held that notice to one carrier participant in an interline move (by means of a claim) is to be considered notice to all of them, and a mere transfer of the claim from one participating carrier to another is not deemed to be legally the equivalent of filing a new claim.[5]

---

5 *Olsen v. R. Co.*, 250 F. 372, and numerous other cases to the same effect.

Index

A

Accidents, 39
Acquisition cost, 129
Act of God, 3, 9, 25, 68, 77, 140
Act of public authority, 9, 33, 68, 77
Act of public enemy, 3, 9, 31, 68, 77
Act of shipper, 9, 35, 69, 77
Actual value rates, 103
Administrative costs, 159
Admiralty Court, 71
Admiralty law, 186
Advisory costs, 159
Agricultural cooperative associations, 62
Air carriers, 9, 31, 62, 75, 88, 91, 99, 165, 176, 185, 193
Airbills, 76, 84, 91, 110
Alcohol, tax on, 153
All-risk insurance, 73
Allowances, 149
Allowances, promotional, 150
Allowances, trade, 150
American Arbitration Association, 198
American Movers Conference, 199
Antiques, 130
Appraised value, 130
Arbitration, 197
Art objects, 129
Association of American Railroads, 198
Average value rule, 76
Aviation Act of 1978, 75

B

Bailee, 1, 55
Bailee, ordinary, 3, 10, 11, 18, 20, 40, 76, 92, 93
Bailments, law of, 1, 54
Bailor, 1
Bankrupt carriers, 209
Bareboat charter, 71
Bill of lading, 13, 16, 40, 84, 91, 98, 108, 110, 112, 115, 146, 164, 167, 171, 193
Bills of Lading Act, 14, 40
Blizzards, 26
Bonds, surety, 201
Boxcar service, 63
Bracing, 39
British law, 5, 25, 53, 61
Brokers, 14, 72, 88, 172, 176, 201
Burden of proof, 54, 67, 69, 189
Bureau of Alcohol, Tobacco and Firearms, 153

C

C.O.D., 146
Carmack Amendment, 59, 62, 141
Carriage of Goods by Sea Act, 65, 88, 175, 176, 185
Cash discounts, 150
Choice of rates, 101
Civil Aeronautics Board, 75, 165
Civil commotions, 69
Civil disturbances, 92

Claim, form of, 167
Claims for uncertain amounts, 169
Claims, carrier handling of, 179
Claims, electronic transmission, 167
Claims, filing of, 167, 204
Claims, time limits, 61, 107, 175, 212
Clear and convincing evidence, 192
Coercion, 38
Coggs v. Bernard, 3, 5
COGSA, 65, 88, 175, 176, 186
Collecting claims, 159
Commercial zones, 62
Common carrier obligation, 12
Common purveyor, 2, 91
Comparative negligence, 10, 93
Compensated intercorporate hauling, 62
Compromise, 180
Computer records, 131
Concealed loss and damage, 43, 71, 113
Confiscation, 33
Congress, U.S., 6
Consequential damages, 28, 118, 122, 142, 143, 161
Consolidators, 88
Constructive placement, 16, 21
Containerized freight, 67, 70, 82
Contamination, 48, 137
Contiguous municipalities, 62
Contraband, 33
Contract carriage, 91, 176, 177, 186
Contract of carriage, 16, 84, 91, 193

Contracts, 75, 88, 91, 99, 139, 198
Contributory negligence, 51, 70
Conversion, 55, 145, 146
Corrosion, 47
Cosmetic damage, 136
Criminal action, 103
Criminals, 31
Customs, 33
Cyclones, 26

D

Damage, cosmetic, 136
Damages, consequential, 28, 118, 122, 142, 143, 161
Damages, punitive, 121
Damages, special, 110, 118, 122, 142, 143, 161, 193
Damages, speculative, 121, 126, 142
Decay, 47
Deductibles, 93, 104
Defective equipment, 28
Delay, 50, 73, 139
Delivery, 106, 124, 168
Delivery appointments, 18, 21, 140
Delivery receipt, 108, 112, 115, 193
Delivery schedules, 139
Delivery, actual, 15
Delivery, duty to accept, 18, 134
Delivery, guaranteed, 140
Delivery, inside, 16
Delivery, refusal, 19, 135, 146
Delivery, tender, 15, 18
Depreciation, 47
Depreciation allowance, 128
Derailments, 39
Deterioration, 142

INDEX

Deviation, 67
Discounts, 149
Discounts, cash, 150
Discounts, promotional, 150
Discounts, trade, 149
Discounts, volume, 149
Discovery, legal right of, 197
Diversion and reconsignment, 24
Documents, 131
Dray service, 66, 80
Driver logs, 193
Drop trailer service, 12, 16
Drying, 47

E

Earthquakes, 26
Effervescence, 47
Electronic data interchange, 168
Elkins Act, 204, 207, 209
Embargoes, 12, 100
Equipment, defective, 28
Estoppel, 97, 99
Evidence, 44, 111, 189, 197
Evidence, clear and convincing, 192
Evidence, preponderance of, 192
Excess valuation, 76
Excess value, 164
Excise taxes, 153
Exemptions, regulatory, 62
Exhibit materials, 165

F

F.O.B. terms, 19, 125, 127
Federal Maritime Commission, 88
Fermentation, 47
Fifteen-day rule, 113
Filed rate doctrine, 180, 211

Fire, 25, 49, 52, 68
Floods, 26, 27, 28, 140
Force majeure, 28, 92
Fraud, 40, 103
Freight bill, original paid, 171
Freight charges, included in claim, 155
Freight charges, on replacement shipment, 157
Freight charges, payment of, 14
Freight charges, set-off against, 203, 209
Freight forwarders, 14, 59, 72, 85, 87, 165, 172, 176
Fumigation, 136
Furs, 130

G

General average, 69, 70
God, act of, 3, 9, 25, 68, 77, 140
Gold franc, 78
Guaranteed delivery, 140
Guatemala Protocol, 79

H

Hague Rules, 65, 88
Hamburg Rules, 72
Harter Act, 65
Hawaii, 65
Hazardous goods, 116
Heating, 47
Heirlooms, 131
Hijacking, 126
Himalaya clauses, 66
Holt, Lord, 3, 5, 57
Household goods, 23, 99, 129, 156, 160, 165, 199
Household Goods Transportation Act of 1980, 160, 199
Hurricanes, 26, 27

I

Ice storms, 140
Igloos, 83
Impact recorders, 111, 194
Implied warranty, 39
Impounded goods, 33
In rem suits, 71, 72
Indemnity bond, 171
Infestation, 48, 137
Inherent vice, 10, 47, 69, 77
Insects, 48
Inside delivery, 16
Inspection, 115
Inspection, cost of, 137
Insurance, 73, 76, 93, 130, 184, 210
Interest, 151
Interline claims, 60
Interline service, 13, 14, 59, 172, 211
Intermodal service, 81
International Monetary Fund, 79
Interstate Commerce Act, 12, 14, 59, 60, 61, 84, 88, 101, 141, 175, 180, 204
Interstate Commerce Commission, 6, 12, 44, 52, 62, 93, 100, 143, 175, 179, 185, 201, 203, 206, 211
Intrastate transportation, 62, 176
Invoice value, 124, 149, 171, 193

J

Jewelry, 130
Joint and several liability, 14, 59, 79, 84, 172, 211
Judicial precedent, 5
Just-in-time, 163

K

Kanban, 163

L

Labor costs, 163
Labor strikes, 29, 69, 92
Land-bridge, 71, 83
Law of bailments, 54
Law-enforcement officials, 33
Lawsuits, time limits, 61, 107, 177, 206
Legal costs, 159, 198
Legal costs, recovery of, 199
Lemon laws, 162
Liability, beginning of, 11, 66
Liability, end of, 15, 66
Liability, limitation, 66, 70, 72, 76, 97, 193
Lien of carrier, 145
Lightning, 26, 52
Limitation of liability, 66, 70, 72, 76, 97, 193
Liquidated damages, 141
Liquor, tax on, 153
Loading, 35, 193
Loss leaders, 127
Loss of sale, 163

M

Manifest, 110, 193
Market value, 123
Marketing premiums, 127
Marking, 39, 69, 111
Micro-bridge, 71, 83
Mini-bridge, 71, 83
Misdelivery, 54, 145
Misdescription, 40, 41
Misrouting, 54
Motor-for-air service, 62
Multi-Transport Operator, 73

INDEX

Multimodal Transport Convention, 73

N

National Freight Claim Council, 198, 203, 206
National monuments, 62
National Motor Freight Classification, 45, 100, 113, 115, 119
National parks, 62
Negligence, 3, 10, 18, 27, 51, 53, 68, 70, 76, 77, 92, 104, 135, 191
Negligence, comparative, 10, 93
Negligence, contributory, 51, 70
Newspaper distribution service, 62
"No-fault" liability system, 7
Non-vessel-operating common carriers, 72, 87

O

Objets d'art, 129
Ocean carriers, 5, 9, 31, 65, 82, 84, 88, 176, 185
On-hand notice, 146
Ordinary bailee, 3, 10, 11, 18, 20, 40, 76, 92, 93
Original value, 133
Owner-operators, 62

P

Packaging, 35, 69, 113, 115
Packaging, damage to, 134
Pairs or sets, 130
Palletized freight, 43, 111
Parcel carriers, 11, 99

Perishable goods, 47, 116, 135, 142
Photographs, 112, 116, 130, 131, 194
Piggyback service, 63, 83
Pilot error, 77
Pilot logs, 193
Pomerene Act, 14, 40
Precedent, judicial, 5
Preponderance of evidence, 192
Product liability, 118
Production line, shutdown, 163
Profit, 124, 158
Promotional allowances, 150
Promotional discounts, 150
Proof beyond a reasonable doubt, 192
Proof, burden of, 54, 67, 69, 189
Protective service, 47, 54, 77, 110, 193
Public authority, act of, 9, 33, 68, 77
Public enemy, act of, 3, 9, 31, 68, 77
Puerto Rico, 65
Punitive damages, 121
Putrefaction, 47

Q

Quarantine, 69

R

Rail car placement, 12
Rate circulars, 16, 21, 44, 76, 78, 99, 139, 146
Reasonable care, 27
Reasonable dispatch, 139
Reconsignment, 20, 24

Recoopering, 133, 136
Recyclables, 134
Redelivery, 21
Regulatory exemptions, 62
Released rates, 97, 157, 193
Repackaging, 133, 136
Repair, 116, 133, 155, 171
Repair costs, 135
Repair, enhancement of value, 136
Repair, overhead allowance, 136
Repair, profit, 136
Replacement cost, 127
Replacement shipments, 124
Res ipsa loquitor, 195
Riots, 29, 69, 92
Road-railer service, 83
Roll On/Roll Off, 82
Rush annotation, 163
Rusting, 47

S

Sabotage, 31, 69, 92
Sale of goods by carrier, 146
Sale, loss of, 163
Sales taxes, 153
Salvage, 117
Salvage allowance, 118
Salvage value, 133, 135
Seal, 110, 195
Seasonal goods, 142
Second-hand goods, 128
Self-insurance, 93, 201
Sentimental value, 131
Set-off, 203, 209
Sets or pairs, 130
Shipper's load and count, 40
Shipper, act of, 9, 35, 69, 77
Shippers National Freight Claim Council, 198, 203, 206
Shippers' agents, 14, 85, 88

Shipping instructions, 13, 20, 23, 66, 146
Silverware, 130
Skids, 43, 111
Slipsheets, 43, 111
Small-claims courts, 186
Snowstorms, 26, 140
Special damages, 110, 118, 122, 142, 143, 161, 193
Special drawing rights, 79
Speculative damages, 121, 126, 142
Spontaneous combustion, 47
Staggers Rail Act of 1980, 6, 52, 63, 140, 175, 185, 186
Statutes of limitations, 177, 184
Stevedores, 66
Stoppage *in transitu,* 24, 56, 146
Storage, 23
Storms, 26, 140
Stowage, 67, 110
Surety bonds, 201

T

Tariffs, 16, 21, 37, 44, 75, 78, 98, 99, 113, 115, 139, 146, 179, 211
Taxes, 153
Temperature recorders, 111, 194
Terrorism, 31, 69, 92
Theft, 126, 145, 147
Third parties, 14, 66, 85, 87, 105, 172, 176
Thunderstorms, 26
Tidal waves, 26
Time limits, 61, 107, 175, 206, 212
Tobacco products, tax on, 153
TOFC service, 63

INDEX

Tornadoes, 26
Tort, 103, 143, 147
Trace, 106, 169
Trade allowances, 150
Trade discounts, 149
Traffic World magazine, 28, 36, 203
Trailer-on-flat-car service, 83
Transit, 24
Transportation Arbitration Board, 198
Treasury Department, U.S., 154

U

Uncertain amounts, claims for, 169
Undercharges, 211
United Nations Conference on Trade and Development, 73
Unloading, 16, 35, 109, 193
Unloading, coercion, 17
Used goods, 128
Usual and customary time, 139

V

Venue, 186
Vermin, 48, 116
Videotapes, 112
Virgin Islands, 65
Virtual insuror, 2, 9, 52, 54, 92, 93
Vis major, 27, 28
Visby Amendments, 72
Volume discounts, 149

W

War, 31, 68
Warehouseman's liability, 6, 10, 11, 23, 40, 76, 92, 119
Warranty, implied, 39
Warsaw Convention, 77, 88, 175, 176, 185
Wastage, 69
Windstorms, 26, 140

Y

York-Antwerp Rules, 70